I0712058

SPIRITUALITY & PSYCHOLOGY

Spiritual Integration in Counseling Psychology
"The Hidden Subconscious Healing Power of the Human Spirit"

Dr. Sam Youssef Ph.D.

Balboa Press books may be ordered through booksellers or by contacting:

Balboa Press
A Division of Hay House
1663 Liberty Drive
Bloomington, IN 47403
www.balboapress.com
844-682-1282

Print information available on the last page.

ISBN: 979-8-7652-2738-1 (sc)
ISBN: 979-8-7652-2740-4 (hc)
ISBN: 979-8-7652-2739-8 (e)

Library of Congress Control Number: 2022906847

Balboa Press rev. date: 04/14/2022

Contents

Acknowledgments

I would love to thank and express my gratitude to my loving and inspiring wife Heba Youssef, my sons Maro and Malek, and my sweet daughter Loujain, without whom this book would not have been possible. Thanks to my soul partner and my great kids for their contributions to my inspiration, knowledge, and other assistance in the writing of this book. Through my life journey, I have come a long way and have learned a tremendous amount of knowledge, which helped me finally reach my own vision of knowledge and wisdom. Without these experiences and lessons of life, this book would not be possible.

I also have a deep appreciation for my colleagues and professors at Grand Canyon University and the talented team of University of Sedona for all the tools that have made this writing process a deeply rewarding experience. Finally, I would like to express my sincere appreciation to the guiding star behind this book, Rev. Dr. Lynda R. Exley, Ph.D. who supported me through her tremendous knowledge, guidance, and kindness.

Sam Youssef Ph.D.
Fort Wayne, Indiana
2021

Introduction

While working as a therapist for many years before having my illustrious career shift to the field of research psychology, and through working with individuals who were suffering from pain both physically and mentally, I became interested in psychosomatic pain. I found psychology to be the most fascinating of all the sciences I studied. While conducting my study as a research psychologist, I came to believe that psychology serves as a bridge between the human spirit and our minds. When it comes to understanding how our ideas, words, and actions are influenced by our thoughts and the mental processes that take place in our brains, physiology is the best place to start. Therapists employ counseling as one of the most essential therapeutic methods for dealing with psychological issues. For this therapeutic technique to work, the therapist must be enthusiastic about the therapeutic healing relationship that he or she and the client have. Soul care was mostly, if not entirely, the responsibility of the clergy for many decades. However, in the last several decades, there has been a dramatic increase in the number of occupations claiming to do soul healing in North America. The standard known main soul care disciplines are Christian counseling, pastoral counseling, biblical counseling, and spiritual direction. These four fields of study are unique, yet they interact with one another and have many of the same underlying ideals.

Therapy that focuses on the whole person is essential. It has been a long time since the field of counseling therapy recognized the need for addressing spiritual and religious issues. Spirituality is increasingly a major consideration in both diagnosis and therapy. Many publications and essays on spiritual and religious principles in counseling are evidence of this interest. Yet counselors ask every question about a client's life, but rarely ask about the effect and significance of spirituality and religion. Because spirituality is rarely discussed in therapy, clients may think that it is not important to their treatment. The main professional organizations for counselors are beginning to acknowledge the significance of spiritual matters. In secular environments, spiritual and religious issues can be therapeutically meaningful, morally suitable, and significant. There are several challenges that counselors face when collaborating with their clients. When a client's religion or spirituality is an issue, it can also be a factor in their recovery. It is important to recognize that spiritual and religious beliefs may play a key role in people's lives, and they should not be overlooked in treatment. Assessing a client's beliefs and behaviors might provide a valuable starting point for further investigation.

Following my studies of parapsychology and metaphysical sciences and through many years of clinical practice in the field of therapy, I was pulled deeper into the spiritual dimension of healing. It is my belief that adding spirituality in the counseling process would lead to a greater sense of humility, compassion, and forgiveness, as well as divine healing that always comes directly from God. In this book, I will examine the developing role of spirituality in counseling psychology by analyzing several counseling programs that use the combination of spiritual and psychological/mental counseling methods in counseling clients, and behavioral shifts that have occurred because of integrating spirituality and psychology. In addition, this book asserts that this integrated approach to counseling psychology causes momentous changes in the human subconscious mind. People have bodies and souls, according to the teachings of religions. The human life is made up of the components that make up the human body, and these parts follow their own nature.

Emotional and psychological components of human existence are intertwined, and each has its own set of requirements. Human souls coexist with the human body, and consequently, must be nurtured. The psycho-spiritual approach is not just applicable to traditional theories of human development; it also touches on the spiritual part of the human being to sort things out. Spiritual guidance and conventional psychology are combined to form the psycho-spiritual method. An individual's spiritual and psychological well-being is also supported in this way. This notion is geared for young people who are still on their way to adulthood. I am not first to take this method, but I want to make it more relatable to the younger generation.

We shall uncover a hidden healing pattern throughout human history: the development of world faiths and spirituality that demand humans acknowledge that they are inadequate and insufficient without connecting with the central divine essence of this universe, God. As counselors, we may use this idea to better grasp the entire range of human emotional well-being. As a result, this person's emotional well-being will be built on a keen sense of self. This method aims to improve the link between the human and divine consciousness by increasing awareness of human needs and limits. Using spiritual tools like prayers, affirmations, meditation, humility, and forgiveness, a more successful psychological therapy can help people improve their emotional and mental well-being by connecting them more to the divine wisdom of human existence. A strong link between humans and God, a profound faith in the divine spirit that manifests itself in many parts of life, such as a strong feeling of self-confidence, honest relationships with others, and an overall sense of well-being, has been found in recent psychological research.

To be true to our therapeutic commitment as healers, therapy should be an ongoing, trusting relationship in which the counselor is committed to doing everything in his or her power to help the client reach his or her full potential mentally and psychologically.

Counseling interventions that can help people connect to their higher mind in a way that helps them improve their overall emotional and mental energy have been linked to the spiritual dimension of consciousness, which has unfortunately been overlooked in our fast-paced industrial and high-tech society of the last century. People become happier and more balanced as they begin to connect with their higher consciousness. Researchers have shown that those who are more spiritually linked and interested in connecting to their higher minds are healthier, less sad, and more confident than their counterparts who are not connected spiritually. This is what we call the faith factor. Studying counseling psychology programs in depth was a wonderful way for me to prove that incorporating the spiritual aspect into the counseling process can help people achieve their ultimate full mental health. Individuals improve by connecting to God and the divine higher intelligence both consciously and subconsciously, and by learning that faith teaches us who we are and what our true meaning in this world is. This is going to be my message in this book.

1

Psychology, Religion, and Spiritual Counseling

Spirituality and religious beliefs may provide a significant source of meaning and purpose in one's life. Religion may not be a major factor in some people's lives, but a personal spirituality may play a significant role. Many individuals find spiritual principles helpful in making sense of the cosmos and the purpose of our lives here on earth. Religious teachings or spirituality, like any other potential source of meaning, appear most real and meaningful when they help us become as completely human as possible. Using them can help us discover our own abilities to think, feel, decide, and act. Many clients rely on religion and spirituality for their sense of purpose in life, and these elements can play a key role in their overall health and well-being. Growing data suggests that our spiritual values and activities may have positive impacts on our physical and mental health. Therapy can be enhanced by incorporating an exploration of these core beliefs with clients. Institutionalized spirituality is religion. As a result, there exists a variety of religious traditions, beliefs, and doctrines. They provide a variety of community-based worship opportunities. All these religions have a similar thread of spirituality. Religions may lose their spirituality if they become institutions of tyranny rather than agents of compassion, peace, and harmony. Instead of uniting the community, they might divide it. This has happened before, as we see in the human history. In the name of faith, more blood has been spilled than for any other cause. Examples include Europe's medieval holy wars, modern-day religious terrorism, and other conflicts. We must not lose sight of the fact that religious organizations exist to help us cultivate our own personal spirituality. Periodic revivals are needed to instill spirituality in the individuals and the community.

As a rule, counseling is a service in which a person or group of people are given advice or direction. Such a service is known as spiritual counseling when the advice or assistance offered is based on spiritual concepts and practices. A large or structured religion is not necessary in this case. Simply associating the advantages of spirituality with desired changes in one's life may be all that is needed. Two common reasons for seeking therapy are well known and commonly documented in psychology literature. Someone may be trying to overcome one or more obstacles in life. Substance misuse or mental health issues might be among them. Because of this, it is possible that the individual may wish to make a modification or improvement. This might be in the form of a promotion or a spiritual awakening. Counseling is a valuable resource in each of these circumstances because it helps people find and overcome problems. Christianity and Islam are two of the most popular religions that succeeded in applying spiritual-therapy models. In these cases, religious leaders are the ones who provide advice. They rely on religious texts like the Koran and the Bible to guide their actions. However, this is not always the case. Most spiritual counselors are nondenominational in their approach. This shows that they do not believe in or support any religious ideology or belief system. As a result, many counselors claim to be able to collaborate with people regardless of their religious views.

Many spiritual counselors feel that a person's relationship to a higher power may have a positive impact on his or her life. An individual can grow and accomplish in ways previously thought impossible or difficult. For those who are dealing with emotional issues, spiritual therapy is also seen to be beneficial. Spiritual therapy helps people achieve their objectives by supporting the belief that there is a larger power at work in the world. Being aware of the importance of this might enable people to realize that they may be more successful overall by relying less on their own efforts and more on the bigger power. When it comes to spiritual therapy, there are several avenues to choose from. Clients have the choice of meeting with a spiritual counselor in person or in a group setting. Telephonic and video conference services are also available from certain religious counselors. A wide range of resources is accessible in the form of books, CDs, and DVDs.

A counselor's ability to assist clients in connecting with others, going beyond themselves, and contributing to the greater good may be eased by incorporating spirituality and religion into counseling. Positive interpersonal relationships, as well as social and community involvement, are commonplace among religious people. As an alternative, persons who are spiritual choose to engage in activities such as self-improvement, creativity, and knowledge building to cultivate their spirituality. Clients' well-being can be improved by counselors who appreciate the importance of religion in their lives. Stress management is favorably correlated with religious and spiritual practices. Religion and/or spirituality alter the way clients appraise distressing events in their lives by giving meaning to life, giving them a stronger sense of control over conditions, and developing self-esteem. In times of stress, religious institutions may provide members with a feeling of community and a sense of identity. Faith in God and the clergy is one of the most widely used religious resources when people are under stress.

Other religious resources include solitary activities and prayer. Dr. Paul Masters the great metaphysical and spiritual thinker, and through his many studies, have shown that religious and spiritual resources may help a wide range of people. He confirmed that religion and spirituality always have a positive influence on the health of people whose income falls below the national average, researchers discovered (Masters, 2012). By offering tools to cope with stress, boost social support, and aid in the discovery of a sense of completeness, religion has served as a source of comfort and strength for those with mental illness. Faster healing and healthier lifestyles can be achieved by those with a strong spiritual identity. To have a healthy spiritual identity, one must feel linked to God's love, experience self-worth, have a sense of purpose and meaning in life, and be able to reach one's fullest potential. In 2016, Cohen revealed that involvement in religion can lessen the risk of impairment in individuals who live in community settings, suggesting that religiosity may play a role in helping people manage physical limitations.

What Is Spirituality?

Spirit is derived from the Latin terms *spiritus* (meaning breath, courage, strength, or soul) and *spirare* (meaning to breathe in and out). Worth, transcendence, connection (to oneself, others, God/supernatural force, and the environment), and becoming better are all qualities of spirituality (the growth and progress in life). It has been at least five decades since the start of spiritual health and its different meanings. Connecting with oneself, others, the environment, and God is the essence of spiritual wellness (transcendental dimension). Spiritual health is characterized by the following: a healthy lifestyle, a sense of community, an inquiry into the meaning and purpose of life, and an ability to transcend. Many academics perceive spiritual health as one of the most significant parts of health, to the point that it is considered one of the most vital elements of mental health. Many studies show that spiritual health improves a patient's mental health as well as his or her physical health, for example, by reducing pain.

Spirituality is often defined as the search for an intrinsic value, but it may also relate to the notion that there is more to life than what we can see on the surface. Spirituality is typically associated with religion; however, the practice of spirituality is often thought to transcend far beyond religion and connect individuals to a higher level of consciousness, an exceptionally unique higher world, such as the infinite world itself. This is when spiritual guidance comes in. Therapists and clients often avoid the issue of spirituality and religion alike because of the possibility for misunderstandings and disagreements over opposing ideas. The incorporation of an individual's spiritual beliefs in the counseling process may aid in the therapeutic process and boost the chance of recovery, according to a study done by Holmes (2005). People's spirituality often takes the form of religion, although in recent years, more people have claimed to be deeply spiritual without subscribing to any religious doctrines or even considering themselves to be religious in any way. Rituals may be part of this type of spirituality. Self-care and concern for others are two of the most common definitions individuals use to characterize spirituality. Others find ways to show their spirituality via spiritual rituals and activities such as yoga, meditation, or even charity work.

Is It Possible to Be Spiritual Without Being Religious?

A person's belief system and customary behaviors about his or her relationship to or with a higher power are both included in definitions of religion and spirituality. A religious theory is normally followed by a particular faith, although spirituality is more open-ended. Due to the lack of established procedures and doctrines in spirituality, it is often less regimented than religion.

We also should be aware that spirituality and religion often share similar characteristics. People's spirituality is typically expressed through religion, for example. Relax, and know that regardless of whether you are spiritual, religious, or a combination of the two, this book will sensitively explore how our personal beliefs play a key role in our psychological well-being. It is thus acceptable to refer to the belief in a higher power as spirituality or religion equally in this book.

In reality, and based on many years of spiritual psychology studies, the term spirituality encompasses more than just religion, since it encompasses parts of one's thoughts, feelings, and actions. If you have ever tried to figure out who you are or what your purpose in life is, you may have considered yourself a spiritual person. There are many civilizations and belief systems that believe in the presence of a spirit. A person's connection to others and to oneself can also be described as spirituality in certain situations. Even though individuals may define themselves as spiritual without subscribing to any religious ideas or even having any religious concept, for others, religion is the embodiment of their spirituality. The rites may be performed in a single tradition or a blend of traditions, with differing levels of devotion and engagement in that religion. Spirituality may also be defined as the concern for one's own and others' well-being. Spirituality may be expressed in a variety of ways, including via various forms of dance, yoga, meditation, and volunteer work.

Psychiatry has always held that religion and spirituality have nothing to do with psychiatry. In the minds of psychiatrists for more than a century, religious convictions and behaviors have been viewed as having a psychopathological base. As a mental condition, religion was seen as a symptom. According to Hemmings (2018), Sigmund Freud and Jean Charcot associated religion with neurosis, as did many other psychologists. In the DSM-3 (*Diagnostic and Statistical Manual of Mental Disorders*, Third Edition), it was suggested that religious and spiritual experiences were indications of psychopathology. This, of course, represented religion adversely. According to the published findings of McMinn in 2011, religion and spirituality helped patients cope with the challenges of life, including their diseases. Psychiatrists are increasingly acknowledging the importance of religion and spirituality in the lives of their patients. Many people increasingly recognize the value of spirituality in a person's mental health. For the practice of psychiatry to be successful, Miller and Rollnick (2013) have lately concluded that the need for religious-psychiatric reconciliation is vital. An exclusive group of researchers on psychiatry and spirituality presently exists at the Royal College of Psychiatrists in London. Training on religious and spiritual issues that might affect mental health is mandated by the American College of Graduate Medical Education in its specific criteria for residency training in psychiatry. A section on religion and psychology was recently created within the WPA (World Psychiatrist Association).

Spirituality and general health are interrelated. Spiritual well-being, like physical wellness, refers to the state of one's soul. There is a link between spiritual well-being and religious belief. The natural world may be a source of spiritual well-being for certain people. For some, their ties to others define it. By living a meaningful life following their own principles, some people cultivate spiritual well-being. Regardless of how spiritual well-being is defined, it entails a relationship between individuals and a larger power. This might be a higher force, a person's personal sense of meaning and purpose, or ideals or belief systems that he or she holds dear. Total well-being encompasses not just physical health but also mental, emotional, and spiritual well-being. A lack of well-being in one part of one's life might have an impact on other aspects of one's health. People with chronic health conditions, for example, may not have a positive outlook on their own health. They may struggle to find purpose in life if they are unable to work, enjoy hobbies, or take care of everyday tasks on their own. Depression or anxiety may be worsened by these sensations.

As a metaphysician, a researcher in spiritual sciences, and a spiritual counselor, I am a firm believer in the concept of spiritual integration in mainstream psychology. In the last twenty years, this movement toward an experiential spirituality in psychotherapy and counseling psychology had shown marked promising outcomes on improving the human mental health. Sound mental health proved to be anchored by spiritual growth based on my experience as a spiritual counselor. This spiritual growth needs to be true to all human values and morals that are deeply rooted in our many religions and ancient traditions and cultures. In his book *Psychology, Theology, and Spirituality in Christian Counseling*, Mark McMinn stated in 2011 that "Most of psychologists and mental health counselors do not want to replace their theoretical commitments to behavioral, cognitive, psychodynamic, family systems, and other forms of therapy." Mental health and spiritual counselors are now more involved spiritually with their clients. We, as counselors and clients, as McMinn explained, need to know more about the deeper side and dimension of life—the spiritual dimension—and connect it to the divine wisdom presented in God in order to connect on a higher level.

Some individuals believe that spirituality and religion are the same. They are similar, yet they are not identical. If you think of religion as a practice and spirituality as a state, you will get a better sense of the distinction. Even if precise religious practices vary from religion to religion, daily behaviors, such as praying and attending church, are common to all of them. These actions of faith and reverence show people's belief in a higher power. Even if you do not go to church/temple/synagogue/mosque very often, you may still believe in a higher power and do things like this to show your devotion to God. Having an elevated level of spirituality does not always mean you are more religious. There are many ways to think about spirituality. The person's beliefs, values, ethics, and everything else that makes life meaningful is part of this inner energy. Journaling, yoga, or meditation may be used to help people sort through their thoughts and feelings.

Spirituality is widely accepted all over the world. Faith and obedience to an all-powerful higher entity known as God, who governs the cosmos and man's fate, are essential components of this belief system. It encompasses a person's quest for the meaning of existence and a sense of interconnectedness with the rest of the universe. Religion and culture have little bearing on the universality of spirituality. Spirituality, on the other hand, is extremely personal and unique to everyone. It is a special place where we can be ourselves. Love, honesty, patience, tolerance, compassion, and a feeling of attachment are among the virtues that may be cultivated via spirituality, in addition to faith and hope. The non-dominant hemisphere/temporal lobe of the brain may have a role in spiritual ideals and experiences.

Spirituality is typically expressed through a personal connection to one's religious tradition. People may rely on the prayers and beliefs of those of the same faith to keep them going. But spirituality is not a requirement for religious beliefs. Religious traditions and belief in a higher power are not necessary to find purpose in life and connect with the broader universe. Psychiatric health is linked to religious and spiritual beliefs. Some mental health issues can be alleviated if people feel connected and feel like they have a feeling of belonging. Religious abuse and bad ideas can have a detrimental influence on one's mental health. However, Dr. Paul Masters' research in 2012 has shown that religion and spirituality typically encourage beneficial coping mechanisms and excellent mental health. Religion can be harmful in some situations, especially if it reaches an extreme level. Treatment results may be improved by adding a patient's spirituality or religious belief system. Increasingly, counselors are incorporating a client's spiritual or religious convictions into their work.

Spiritual Counseling as a Therapeutic Method

In spiritual therapy, a person's soul, as well as his or her mind and body, is treated by accessing individual belief systems and using that faith in a higher power to examine areas of conflict in the person's life. To others, spiritual counseling might help them connect more deeply with their guiding higher force. A person who is depressed may discover a moral dilemma in some aspect of his or her life because of spiritual counseling. Self-sabotage can cause anxiety if it is done unintentionally. There are many ways to treat conflict and mental health issues, and spiritual therapy is just one of them. However, some people may find it to be a useful paradigm.

Nature therapy, meditation, music, and other unconventional therapeutic techniques can all be incorporated into this approach to foster a deeper connection between the body, mind, and soul, and help the client better understand his or her innermost thoughts and feelings. One's spirituality may have nothing to do with religion but may simply involve a knowledge of the cosmos and one's relationship with it. Individuals who identify as spiritual often express a desire to develop a sense of harmony with the cosmos and will often engage in spiritual treatment to that end.

Spiritual transformation through counseling always involves an awareness of the real meanings of our existence in life, and our relationship with God—an awareness of neediness, as McMinn called it. As McMinn has stated, "A more comprehensive perspective on psychological and spiritual health requires us to consider self, brokenness, and healing relationships as interactive rather than linear." He described a different sense of human self, the sense that will help us to recognize ourselves in relation to God and our responsibilities towards him, combined with our parallel responsibilities to ourselves and to the rest of the world. Having this deeper sense of healthy, sound knowledge of neediness will assure our humble sense and support a higher inner spiritual strength contrary to a natural human tendency towards self-centeredness.

If we believe that the divine Holy Spirit representing almighty God is the basis of all realities and truth, we should not be surprised that the major three perspectives of psychology based on integrative psychotherapy—the functional, structural, and relational—correspond nicely to the three main religious foundations of creation:

sense of self, feeling of need, and redemption. As McMinn (2011) stated in his book "Psychology Theology and Spirituality":

"This should not surprise us, because God is the author of all truth. If theologians and philosophers study the image of God in humans, psychologist study human behavior, it seems reasonable that they would come to some similar conclusion, whether the psychologists acknowledge God as the creator of humanity. This is God's world, and everything we study has God's fingerprints all over it.

If we as researchers review the last fifty years of psychology and psychiatry's literature, we will see that both sciences have dealt extensively with most mental illness issues, such as anxiety, depression, addiction, and abuse. On the other hand, we have not dealt with the foundations of mental health, such as meaning and purpose of human existence, positive feelings, emotions, motivation, and achievement of positivity in relationships. That was one of the main reasons that, in the last twenty years, there was a clear shift in the way we looked at mental health. From a spiritual point of view, we need the kind of psychology that can be based on positivity (the birth of positive psychology), which can enhance authentic positive dimensions of both psychological and spiritual health; we cannot look only on the healing mental aspect but must also include the presence of the divine element of God in our souls and reflect that in our relationships.

The approach of psychology to mental healing has already passed through several distinct stages. If we reduce these stages to the simplest interventions, we begin with mesmerism, which developed later into hypnotism. Next was mental suggestion which led, finally, to mental explanation, the method employed presently by most psychologists. Neither psychiatry nor psychotherapy is hypnotic, and neither practice includes mental suggestion. The entire field is one of explanation. In psychotherapy, the explanation is drawn from the patient's consciousness in such a way that he or she sees his or her trouble, and by this self-seeing, the difficulty is supposed to be dissipated. E. Holmes explained these topics more in his book "Living the Science of Mind." He proved that in the earliest stages of psychotherapy, it was thought necessary that the psychotherapist should draw out of the consciousness of his or her patient every trivial incident which might have led to his or her mental and physical undoing. He added, "This has made of psychoanalysis/psychotherapy one of the most subtle of arts, as well as one of the most difficult practices. If one expects to draw out of the consciousness of one's patient the most trivial incidents of his life, the method becomes painstaking, laborious, and cumbersome; then the treatment must cover an extended period."

Some people or families may have strong religious or spiritual belief systems and devote substantial parts of their lives to them. A person's self-care regimen may include religious or spiritual activities, such as going to church or volunteering in the community. A person's spiritual beliefs can have a considerable impact on how he or she copes with life's challenges. Social and emotional support, meaning and purpose in life, bereavement relief, and ethical and moral norms are all outcomes of spiritual activities. People who are religious or spiritual may receive help from therapists who are more sensitive to their religious or spiritual beliefs, since this may inspire them to consider a larger range of therapy options.

People in therapy may receive help from materials provided by therapists who are aware of therapeutic procedures rooted in spirituality, such as spiritual journaling and forgiveness protocols. People who draw their power from their spiritual beliefs may struggle to develop and heal in therapy if they are not able to include their entire selves in the process. Many twelve-step programs are based on the conviction and faith in a higher power, even if this power is not explicitly mentioned in the program's philosophy. People's anxiety, tension, and tolerance for ambiguity were shown to be influenced by their spiritual views, according to a C.G.Young (2010). A belief in a higher power was found to have a positive effect on trust, stress levels, and intolerance in individuals. According to McMinn (2011), those who are struggling with substance misuse may receive help from spiritual treatment.

In spirit/mind healing, we do not have to uncover every unconscious cause of mental confusion with its attendant physical distress. We know that broad, generalized statements often affect a healing of disease without either the practitioner or the patient having any specific knowledge of its cause. We know that the clearer one's consciousness is, and the more definitely certain one is that Spirit is the absolute cause of all and that good alone governs, the more quickly healing will take place. As Holmes (2005) stated in the same book, "We know that silent recognition and realization elevate the consciousness to a place of greater power and make possible a more immediate manifestation. Jesus did not analyze people in his society". Positive spiritual psychology focuses on the true, honorable, right, pure, lovely, and admirable, and on the divine image in humanity. Integrating positive spiritual psychology in recent years has shown that faithful and grateful people are happier, healthier, less depressed, and more self-confident than others. We all can see the key role of positive spiritual psychology in developing the true feeling of self and the sense of need; the mission of spiritual counselors is to share this healing journey sincerely with clients as they transform themselves to a higher level of both psychological and spiritual health.

Discovering the Spiritual Identity

The process of discovering one's spiritual self is essential to spiritual therapy and healing. According to the traditional definition of spiritual guidance, one person supports another's spiritual growth. Also, a "sense of direction" can be used more generally to describe a stage of spiritual development in which one feels guided on a journey or discovers one's destiny. Many shades of meaning can be conveyed based on the environment in which spiritual development and counseling is used, from formal to informal and professional to casual.

There are many ways to define spiritual guidance and, for the development of one's inner life, a spiritual mentor, or counselor, or coach may be necessary to achieve this kind of guidance.

Spiritual guidance can be based on these principles.

- Experience and awareness are gradually revealed through an internal process.
- Conversations with a contemplative tone might assist a person figure out his or her own way.
- Friendship through the joys and hardships of the spiritual path is referred to as soul friendship or partnership.

A person's individual circumstances influence which of these interpretations is most relevant to that person. The format changes depending on the amount of formality. Like other types of therapy, spiritual guidance is provided on an ongoing basis in individual sessions. Formal spiritual guidance is looked for by individuals for a wide range of reasons. When it comes to certain people, it is a natural response to their need for growth and expansion. During big life transformations, many people turn to spiritual assistance and guidance. Motives can come from a wide variety of sources. Initial discussions can evaluate whether formal spiritual guidance is necessary in a certain scenario.

This type of counseling does not focus on fixing issues, unlike psychotherapy or mental health counseling. In spiritual direction and guidance, the focus is primarily on finding and reacting to one's spirit's leadings and cultivating a more authentic state of being. Before spiritual guidance may be effective, psychotherapy may be needed. Acutely distressed or mentally ill individuals should look for medical and psychiatric help first. Although spiritual guidance may be a useful part of holistic therapy, it is best used in conjunction with other health practices.

Counseling/Talk Therapy for Spiritual Development

Spiritual growth can be seen as a progression of phases. To understand the phases of faith formation, Erik Erikson's popular stages of lifetime development might be applied according to Hemmings (2018). For those who believe in God's integrity, or those who feel God's lack of reliability has left them feeling depressed and hopeless, this is a critical stage. For this first stage to be resolved, one must have a renewed sense of hope in God and a deeper confidence in the godly plan for his or her life. Adulthood in Erikson's paradigm would correspond to Erikson's last phase of spiritual growth. This is the stage where a person has reached a level of spiritual maturity and knowledge via his or her own personal growth. During these latter phases of growth, this individual would serve as a mentor and advisor.

The purpose of spiritual counseling/coaching is to help clients develop spiritually. Working through hurdles like distrust, shame, doubt, self-condemnation, and feelings of insecurity and loneliness may be overcome via spiritual therapy and coaching. Counselors and coaches who specialize in spiritual development can find a client's stage of faith development and work with the client to help him or her grow spiritually by building the client's trust, strengthening his or her ability to resist evil and negative influences, clarifying the client's divine purpose, developing his or her spiritual tools, and encouraging completion of tasks that serve God's purposes. There are actual results when counseling/coaching and spiritual guidance come together. God is at work. Spiritual counseling/coaching may help people reach a better knowledge of themselves and the world around them, as well as a greater appreciation for God's work.

◆ 2 ◆

Spiritual Counseling as an Old and New Psychotherapeutic Profession

Emotional healing and progress can be achieved under the guidance of a spiritual counselor. It is common to see people struggling to find a sense of purpose or meaning in their lives. Getting the skills necessary to practice spiritual counseling can be particularly challenging. Potential spiritual counselors may be learning how to cope with sadness and anguish. When it comes to incorporating spirituality into their work, counselors' spiritual journeys are just as diverse as those of their clients. From Judaism and Christianity to Islam and Buddhism, there are a variety of religions. If you are looking for a spiritual counselor, you may want to look for someone who does not adhere to the strict doctrines of his or her faith. To be a successful spiritual counselor, you must be a good listener, empathetic, caring, perceptive, and spiritually aware. In addition, spiritual counselors can include other forms of therapy into their practice. It is common for the phrase "spiritual counselor" to be used to refer to a wide range of approaches to spirituality. It might be orthodox, or it could be more mystical, new age, or Native American-inspired. If you are looking for a spiritual counselor, you may or may not need to search for a degreed spiritual counselor. For a spiritual counselor, training in typical therapy methods may not be necessary.

There are millions of people who suffer from mental illness, which may have a significant impact on their lives and well-being. According to Cohen (2016), the World Health Organization (WHO) estimates that one in four people will suffer from mental illness at some point in their lives. The world has lately seen a rise in the number of cases of mental illness, which is why recent data indicates a greater rate than in the past. This shows the need to look at the efficacy of interventions and implement some strategies to deal with these kinds of situations. Spiritual therapies, on the other hand, have gained popularity among a wide range of medically ill patients as well as healthy persons worldwide, and their efficacy has been proved. In spiritual counseling, the counselor focuses on the patient's spirituality and seeks to assist the patient in dealing with his or her problems, with an emphasis on spiritual themes. Techniques include prayer, forgiveness, helping others, taking notes in a journal, book therapy, worshipping, and spiritual imagery. This counseling has been proven to be beneficial in altering people's unproductive attitudes. As an example, McMinn (2011) have pointed to the need of pastoral counselors and religious experts in providing these services. According to Lipton (2016), research psychologists in the United States recently conducted a study on cancer patients and decided that medical doctors should introduce these patients to pastoral counselors who specialize in religious problems since the patients' brains are occupied with their religious views.

The relevance of religious experts in providing spiritual therapies for cancer patients was also emphasized by the same study. Mental health care professionals and counselors have also been included in certain mental health care programs as potential suppliers of spiritual counseling services. It is important for the counselor to urge the client to talk about his or her religious or spiritual beliefs with the counselor while the client is feeling irritated since the client is more likely to do so when the client can vent his or her feelings. Modern health care programs focuse on how health care workers, such as nurses, can assist patients with both physical and mental health issues in the hospital. Nurses, who play a critical role in calming and supporting patients with mental health issues, are a suitable alternative for presenting spiritual counseling to those who are hospitalized since they build relationships with patients.

Counselors and psychologists play a key role in spiritual care, and according to McMinn (2011), several studies have proven the need of preparing these professionals in the spiritual sector so that they may better serve their diverse clientele. Researchers found also that mystics were competent in delivering spiritual counseling services and educating spiritual counseling students. Aside from their interest and conviction in spiritual matters, spiritual counselors also have a number of other important traits. It is easier to train religious experts in spiritual counseling courses in most of the world's educational systems than to train mental health experts in long-term programs involving religion and spirituality.

The Body/Mind/Spirit Approach

Many of life's difficulties have physical parts, which is acknowledged by spiritual counselors. Many mental and emotional problems may be traced back to the way our bodies are wired, whether because of our genes, sickness, or physical and emotional trauma. Therefore, spiritual counselors should aim to collaborate with doctors who are devoted to understanding both the patient's bodily and spiritual condition. Many doctors are unable to provide their patients with the degree of therapy they look for due to time restrictions. This partnership between doctors and spiritual counselors is a solution where everyone involved benefits.

Spiritual counselors are likewise aware of an increase in public neurological optimism. A chemical imbalance or a genetic flaw is often thought in many medical and mental health professions to be the source of an emotional struggle that cannot be attributed to a particular physical reason (e.g., brain trauma, endocrine dysfunction, tumor, illness, infection, nerve damage). Diagnoses of mental illness are prevalent, and psychiatric drugs are often recommended to treat the symptoms by changing the patient's emotions chemically.

In his book "Theory and Practice of Counseling and Psychotherapy", Corey stated, "It necessitates a practitioner who is willing to be a real person in the therapeutic interaction. The client's progress occurs in the setting of such a person-to-person interaction." Recent studies have shown that the counselor's personality is a critical part of a successful therapeutic interaction. Most clients place more importance on the counselor's personality than they do on the exact tactics used in treatment. As Corey described in the same book: "These strategies are of less value in the therapy process. The spiritual counselor becomes a symbol to the one seeking aid, this symbol in the mind of the client typically signifies knowledge, strength, self-mastery, understanding, insight, and healing." As a result of this exaggeration of the client's perception of a counselor's qualities and talents, most counselors cannot live up to the picture their clients have of them.

Personal Characteristics of a Good Counselor

In a study by Corey in 2018 on this issue, he succeeded in finding the personal characteristics and attributes of a good counselor. Corey explained: "It is important for people to know who they are and what they want out of life, as well as what's most important to them. Help and affection may be exchanged between people who are self-aware and self-confident. If they are not happy with their current situation, they have the bravery and willingness to leave their comfort zone and try something new. These people are mindful of the decisions they made in the past about themselves and others as well as the world.

They do not hide behind tight roles and facades; they are genuine, truthful, and honest. A good spiritual counselor must have a good sense of humor: They can see things from a humorous viewpoint. They have not lost their ability to chuckle at their own mistakes and inconsistencies. While they are not afraid to confess that they have made mistakes, they also do not linger on their failures."

Psychologists and spiritual counselors must work together to help people heal. An experienced psychologist or a mental health counselor should also have an established prayer life to be a successful therapist. In this scenario, too, the counselor needs a spiritual director. In this way, the counselor will be able to better understand his or her own prayer life. A counselor cannot be as successful as he or she could be if the counselor does not understand his or her own prayer life well. The counselor becomes a parent or an elder sibling of the client during the counseling process. This is because the counselor must remember that he or she is a professional, but he or she must also show compassion to the counselee.

Counselors are not obsessed with the past or future; they live in the now. They can share their experiences and be present in the now. They recognize the importance of culture and the effect it has on their lives, and they respect the different values held by people from other cultures. Respect, care, trust, and a true value for others are the foundations of their concern for others' well-being. With good people skills, individuals can enter other people's lives and build collaborative partnerships. Their job becomes meaningful to them, and they can accept financial benefits while without becoming slaves to their profession. The bravery to follow their aspirations and interests is clear in the way they exude an enthusiasm that is contagious. Although they try to be present for their customers, they are still able to set up healthy boundaries and do not carry the issues of their clients about with them during their leisure hours.

Focusing more on this section of my book on the ideal counselor, I have also included a complete list of the characteristics needed to be an effective spiritual counselor based on my views and experience. Approaches to mental health should incorporate both spiritual and psychological elements. If you are looking for a more comprehensive approach to counseling, you will want to investigate spiritual counseling. We, as spiritual counselors, are concerned with the process of spiritual growth and development, as well as positive mental health, in contrast to behaviorist counselors, who focus on reducing symptoms. A common assumption in most psychological and mental health techniques is that mental health is distinct from spiritual health, which most spiritual and Christian counselors deny. Counselors who specialize in spiritual issues feel that mental and spiritual well-being are not mutually exclusive.

What Is the Spiritual Counselor's Purpose?

The therapist cannot lead clients to religious or spiritual practices based on his or her own personal insights. Avoid interfering with clients' spiritual beliefs and discussions that are not directly relevant to the treatment. Most religious and spiritual traditions' ethical precepts may be found in the code of ethics for spiritual counselors. Respect, accountability, sincerity, competence, and consideration for others are a few examples of these virtues. An analyst using a minimalist approach to religion evaluation is unable to distinguish between religious content and psychological content when dealing with a client who has a strong religious and spiritual side. They believe that spiritually inclined analysts can better distinguish between the psychological and spiritual components that clients bring with them to sessions and can employ spirituality more effectively. Psychologists can discuss the psychological impacts of religious/spiritual applications where there is finding in these subjects. This means that the benefits of spiritual psychotherapy should be communicated to the patients. Therapists must adhere to ethical values and respect for others' views to employ these treatments, according to this statement.

Humans have always had a deep-seated need to heal, and this desire can be traced back to the beginnings of time. In human literature, as well as in holy texts, religions, and most social values systems, we find many links to this therapeutic technique. Our understanding of what is good and what is evil is the foundation of this idea. God designed us to have a keen sense of ourselves. If we have this sense of self, we may choose to be someone who is kind and loving or someone who is self-centered. We can also choose to be self-centered or God-centered. Humans, on the other hand, tend to use their God-given freedom of choice without considering the repercussions.

Pain and suffering are often the result of a lack of responsibility in one's profession. By harming others as an example, an adult human expresses his or her willful independence, causing enormous sorrow in many people's lives. It is common for those who prioritize freedom over their duties to experience dire consequences. It is common for humans to live under a false sense of self-sufficiency, and they are often confronted with feelings of perpetual neediness and anguish that have affected human freedom and independence. "Sometimes anguish is generated by personal disobedience; other times profound scars come from the rebellion and sin of others," McMinn said in his book. There is a spiritual essence at the heart of all religions. Simply put, the essence of this philosophy is that spirituality is a relationship with God. Pain and brokenness are requirements to understanding God's grace, according to all spiritual traditions. This is the best time for spiritual counseling and direction since all faiths have spoken about redemption, which supplies hope and purpose to fallen individuals. The basis for spiritual therapy is founded on a basic reality that can be seen in life: human development, profound spiritual growth, and interactive psychological transformation are all part of a natural, continual process.

To understand human growth, we must first understand our ability to distinguish ourselves from others in our early years, and throughout our path of differentiating ourselves, we learn and grow our own autonomy. While autonomy is an important part of human growth, we must also recognize that there is a natural limit to autonomy, and that expected limitation is always characterized by suffering. We look to our parents for guidance, support, and consolation when we are going through hardships like hunger, illness, physical discomfort, or loneliness. In the spiritual realm, we can use the same approach. When we face adversity and hardship, we tend to realize the importance of God's grace and love in our lives.

As a simple pattern of spiritual healing, the process of spiritual change must entail a deep awareness of one's own neediness. We can build a meaningful healing connection with God and others once we admit our brokenness and need. After admitting the helpless and damaged state of our souls, we may experience a shift in our mental state. This pattern of spiritual healing may be seen in McMinn's illustration of a person's psychological transformation: "Addicts in recovery who regularly attend 12-step groups admit their brokenness and join with others in a healing community by attending meetings on a regular basis." The same thing happens at the counseling office from time to time.

When assessing a client's condition and prospective remedies, a spiritual counselor must adhere to a set of principles.

1. Listen attentively to clients

To understand the client's condition, the counselor must be receptive to what the client has to say and refrain from making any snap judgments about it. Because the counselor is either a parent or a sibling, he or she must listen to all that is said.

2. Allow for rationalizations

In therapy, excuses are often not allowed. While the client is free to supply an explanation, the counselor must be able to explore and challenge every conceivable explanation for further information. When confronted with the excuse, the client should feel compelled to show the truth. After that, the client must be processed and educated that speaking the truth would not do any damage.

3. **Never stop trying**

If a client's circumstance needs an outside specialist, the counselor should not give up on him or her in any therapeutic procedure. The psycho-spiritual counselor must continue in contact with the counselee for spiritual direction if the client is sent to someone else.

Religious or spiritual therapies may be necessary in the treatment plan for a client who ranks religion or spirituality as extremely important. Professional therapists who advocate the inclusion of religion in therapy agree that psychology has neglected the vital role that religion plays in the lives of many people; however, they stress that a religious intervention must be practiced in a clinically sensitive, ethically responsible, and professionally competent manner. The use of any spiritual intervention as part of psychotherapy should be approached with caution, according to McMinn. Therapists should not use spiritual treatments to impose a certain religious tradition on their individual clients, but they should always work within the client's value system as far as workable, according to McMinn. Spiritual or religious interventions should only be used with written permission from the client and supervisor (where proper), and parental approval if dealing with minors. Occasionally, a psychotherapist may recommend that the client seek help from a clergy member or other spiritual consultant. The pastor of the client's church may be a reliable source of information on the community's views on divorce and remarriage. The treatment session should not be entirely devoted to the client's spiritual issues. In many cases, it is more suitable for the therapist to propose non-counseling options for the client to try. Prayer, contemplation, and meditation, reading sacred texts, and forgiveness and repentance are some of the therapeutic methods that therapists may propose. In addition to treatment, individuals may also seek spiritual guidance from a variety of sources.

If we look at the Christian model as an example, the spirit-centered model of therapy looks at how God's redemption narrative may be recreated at every level of creation. The Spirit-centered model offers an approach to counseling that is both practical and unique, since it incorporates insights from systems theory, particularly in relation to stages of change, as well as the macro-stories of the Old Testament, particularly as fulfilled in Jesus's mission. Modeling reality in terms of relationships, this paradigm sees the spirit-centered therapist as a manifestation of the Holy Spirit who, in collaborating with clients, looks to partner with the spirit in bringing them into the patterns of God's redemption narrative. Changes of the second and third order take part in this process, in which conventional knowledge is replaced with countercultural wisdom, which Jesus championed and named the Kingdom of God, to transform society. There are epistemological transformations in both the process and the outcome of spirit-centered therapy that allow individuals to perceive and live in the world differently.

Studies show that spirituality may be used to improve one's health and well-being in diverse ways. When faced with difficulties, many people seek solace in religion or other forms of spirituality. Members of historically marginalized groups, for whom spirituality is especially important, tend to feel that it can help them deal with their issues. There is still a lack of trust between practitioners and patients on the value of discussing spirituality. As a subject, spirituality is often treated with great care and discretion. Practitioners, who are typically thought to be secular, are often hesitant to accept religious information from their clients. A comparable scenario exists for those who are regularly misunderstood by the majority culture. For example, a person of African American descent may have comparable worries while engaging with European-American healthcare providers. For therapeutic strengths to be used, trust and rapport must be built.

Considering this concept just presented, spiritual competency is crucial for successful work with spiritually diverse people. It helps practitioners build trust and rapport with their patients. Additionally, spiritual competency aids practitioners in avoiding harmful clinical encounters, accessing the spiritual strengths of patients, and improving clinical results. Practitioners who cultivate spiritual competence will be more prepared to manage the difficulties of dealing with people from varied cultural backgrounds. These advantages show that social workers can gain from enhancing their abilities.

Finding the Right Spiritual Counselor

Finding a professional spiritual counselor can be a challenge. Individuals who have been certified as spirituality therapists are preferred (if you are in a state that recognizes spiritual therapy). To learn more about the experience of dealing with clients who are interested in exploring spirituality and spiritual practices, you may want to talk to multiple therapists, even if your state does not officially recognize this type of therapy. Life coaches are often therapists who specialize in spirituality in places where spirituality therapy is not recognized as a legitimate kind of treatment. The fact that life coaching is unregulated means that anybody may claim to be a life coach, regardless of education or experience. However, this does not imply that all spiritual life coaches are unqualified. As a result, it is imperative that you research the qualifications and work history of anyone with whom you intend to collaborate. As an alternative to finding a spiritual counselor, you may need to seek help from a religious professional of your own faith. Many therapists exist, but they tend to be overbooked and do not give priority to those who only want to learn more about their faith. Grief therapy is an exception to this rule. You can also go to religious organizations for help in the mourning process if you are looking for an alternative to a spiritual counselor.

◆ 3 ◆

The Philosophy of Spiritual Psychology

Anthropology is at the heart of every type of counseling—secular or spiritual. Human beings' ideal condition, the norms for conduct, thoughts, emotions, and intentions, and how to solve problems are all based on these core ideas about humans. These beliefs motivate every endeavor to aid humans. Humans were created as both physical and spiritual beings by direct divine action in the likeness of God so that they may reflect the grandeur of God and require and enjoy an intimate connection with the Creator. Having been created in the image of God and given a divine mission to rule over the rest of the universe differentiates people from all other living forms.

Based on the Old Testament in Christianity, and the verses of Koran in Islam, in the Garden of Eden, Satan's falsehoods about God, about himself, and about the workings of God's creation led to the beginning of humankind's disintegration. The truth of God was exchanged for a deception and disobedience which were committed by humankind. Since then, humankind's wicked responses have been based on trusting someone else's words rather than God's. Humanity was thrust into an alienation from God because of Adam and Eve's transgression. According to the Bible, there was a fundamental shift in the essence of humans away from God, combined with an underlying desire inside to live and rule himself or herself. The terms "flesh" or "sinful nature" refer to this wicked inclination in humans. There was no erasure of the image of God in humans or a diminution in their value as image-bearers before God because of sin. God's image in humans was severely tarnished by this insurrection against God. Since then, God was no longer accurately reflected in humanity.

Because spiritual counselors begin with distinct presuppositions and work from a different worldview, they analyze, assess, and aim to correct dysfunctional thinking, behavior, and emotional states of individuals in a unique way. In the first chapter of Genesis, that worldview and those presuppositions underpin the validity of human inquiry and progress as a part of God's purpose for humans. An entity that is both spiritually ethereal and everlasting, as well as physically material, can only be studied through psychology. A spiritually sensitive observer can discern the precise features of God's grandeur in the nonliving portions of creation (e.g., physics, geology, and astronomy) or in the living components of plants and animals (botany and zoology). Psychology, on the other hand, focuses on the part of creation that bears God's image—the psyche of humans.

For example, secular research does not consider humans' fallen and sinful nature, humans' tendency to censor God from their thoughts, the tendency to worship and serve themselves, or the disturbing effects that unredeemed men and women have when disconnected from God and unable to receive his enabling grace during trials. There are a lot of studies that show a lack of awareness or open disdain of the subject's status as a God-image bearer and the necessity for the subject to know his or her Creator and his teachings to genuinely grow under God's authority in God's universe. A spiritual perspective will therefore skew and grossly misinterpret the findings of such study.

Non-duality, or simple oneness, between the observer and the observed occurs during a spiritual experience. A spiritual experience is defined by emotions of sanctity, tranquility, and happiness, a sense of transcending time and space, and an intuitive belief that the experience is a source of objective truth about the world. It is impossible to overstate the importance of spiritual encounters for those who have them and for the rest of us. On a personal level, spiritual experiences have a profound effect on the characters and values of those who have them. Similarly, on a worldwide scale, spiritual experiences are at or near the origin of religions, and civilization as we know it. A profound human identity may be found in the spiritual origins of our conscious experiences, regardless of ethnic, racial, or religious variations. Our comprehension of these transforming experiences is so critical.

In Buddhism and Hinduism, the notion of spiritual enlightenment is most related. Detachment and mindfulness are two attributes essential to achieving enlightenment. This spiritual concept asserts that life is rife with pain because of the connection of the soul to objects of this world, and that this attachment is inescapable. Thus, a soul is enlightened when it can stay in the world while letting go of its attachments. A person's spiritual journey, whether it spans a single lifetime or several, is said to conclude with enlightenment. Nirvana is the Buddhist term for enlightenment. According to Hinduism, nirvana is described as a state of tranquility and oneness with the universe. The path to nirvana is taught differently in various schools of Buddhism. As an example, orthodox Buddhists closely follow the Four Noble Truths and Noble Eightfold Path. Others, such as Zen Buddhists, may employ tough mental exercises, such as koans (paradoxical statements or questions used as meditation discipline for novices), in their spiritual practices. Practicing meditation on a regular basis is an important part of most Buddhist traditions.

Nirvana is also used in Hinduism as a metaphor for liberation from desire and other impure longings. The end of the Hindu cycle of rebirth also includes spiritual enlightenment. In this religion, the souls of those who have died are reincarnated in many other bodies. They grow spiritually in each of their lifetimes. For those who want to achieve moksha—the goal of this spiritual growth—the notion of spiritual enlightenment is included. Enlightenment is viewed as a mystical idea by most people. As a result, a spiritual clarity that can neither be described in words nor achieved by action is implied. For example, even if you can recite the words of every sage, you would not be enlightened by reading. It is possible for everyone to reach enlightenment, but each person's road to it is unique. However, teachers can aid and challenge their students, but they cannot compel their students to become enlightened.

Buddhism's and Hinduism's concepts of spiritual enlightenment are like yet separate from Christianity's concept of salvation and transcendence. Zen's koan "If you encounter the Buddha while traveling, kill him!" says that enlightenment can only be achieved when one is freed from instructors and doctrines. Furthermore, enlightenment does not need the existence of a separate heaven from Earth. It emphasizes a shift in the way the soul interacts with the material world. As the enlightened one realizes that reality is only an illusion, he or she continues to live a bodily existence. One does not ascend to a distinct place.

Because of God's rule on free will presented in the other major world religions, our actions and decisions are unaffected by what he does or does not allow us to do. If we are unwilling to accept his aid, he will not force it onto us. Only if we are in a life-threatening scenario before our time will we be exempt from this rule. A good spiritual counselor must help the client in reducing the resistance he or she exerts against divine direction. Our lives have been blessed with several instances of divine intervention. Many individuals may not know how God and the angels helped them get to where they are now. They may also believe that God has a hand in their life's notable events. In her book, "Divine Guidance," Dr. D. Virtue stated that the voice of our God has never gone away. "When God first thought of you, a spark of Divine light was ignited within you. You are one with God because the light is one with God. You have access to God's thoughts because of the Divine light, which is genuine essence. Then, in fact, your thinking is forever linked to the Divine knowledge of God's mind," The client will have access to all the answers he needs from a spiritual counselor who is able to assist him connect with the divine mind, and he/she will be able to have a continuous personal guide who is ready to answer all questions, and will have no demands in return. Each of us already has access to this all-knowing advisor.

In Dr. Virtue's words, "When we get into the habit of having continual talks with God, our every action and thought is led with great harmony." Spirituality is mostly an approach to living that is unique to the individual. According to Ernest Kurtz and Katherine Ketcham in their book "The Spirituality of Imperfection", they explained that spirituality of imperfection is a way of life. All aspects of our lives are affected by spirituality because it affects how we view the world, how we feel, and what decisions we make depending on these feelings and beliefs. Spirituality is a three-part experience, what we see, how we feel, and why we select. Spiritually enlightened people are happier and more satisfied with life than persons who do not believe in any religions or sects, regardless of whether they are religious or spiritual. In Tom Butler-Bowdon's "50 Psychology Classics," Martin Seligman explained that "Religious persons have lower rates of depression and are more resilient to setbacks and tragedy. According to one study, the more a person follows his/her religious beliefs, the more positive their outlook on life becomes. People feel better about themselves and the world when they have a keen sense of optimism for the future." It is via this higher level of mind that the divine guidance of God may provide for all individuals' needs, including love, monetary assistance, encouragement, and solid advice; this higher level of mind allows individuals to better connect with their divine higher minds.

Many spiritualists who believe in God passionately believe that the divine source can be readily characterized as pure love, light, and intellect; therefore, if they choose to connect to this godly divine source, they will undoubtedly get all these boundless benefits. It is our job as spiritual counselors, as well as our clients, to teach unspiritual people how to recognize the signals of divine guidance and how to reach out for it in many ways.

There are several ways in which these visions or signals occur to us, such as in the form of mental snapshots. Dreams are also a common way for these visions to take place. It is possible that these symbols, noises, voices, and phrases are both internal and external to the mind, and even sound like our own. Divine direction can also come in the form of thoughts, emotions, and bodily experiences, such as the sense of smell. The innate knowledge, or what I call knowingness, is also another way of divine communication. It is when we get information directly from God's universal divine wisdom through thoughts, concepts, and inner certainties.

God's means of leading our spirits away from suffering and toward serenity is through divine direction. Through the practice of prayer, spiritual counselors share this supernatural source of wisdom with their clients. When we pray to God, we always get a response that incorporates love. A clear answer from God is always given to our prayers. "Divine advice is always centered on helping, healing, and improving," Dr. Doreen Virtue said in the same book. Nothing like scarcity, fear, or competitiveness should be mentioned while connecting with the divine source. According to Virtue and based on the testimonies of many of his clients who attended spiritual counseling sessions, the divine instruction arrives in the form of "soft clouds of confidence" when it is coming from God.

To be spiritually enlightened is to be aware of the interconnectedness of all things—the awareness that we are all connected within the same life matrix. The ideas and feelings we have in our mind are what manifest in our physical existence. Therefore, you may feel linked or disconnected from the results of your belief based on your ideas and feelings. In our physical world, everything we see, hear, taste, and touch is a function of our perceptions. When light enters the eyes, information is sent as neurological signals to the brain, which generates a three-dimensional physical image. There is no such thing as a picture outside of the mind, which is where all thoughts, feelings, and images exist. A person's thoughts and feelings combine to generate an image in his or her mind's eye.

Thought or information, for example, provides the three-dimensional image in your mind's eye when it creates its shape, size, and structure. Color, texture, warmth, taste, smell, and other characteristics are all given by the substance or vibration of the experience itself. The illusion of separation is always the first step or stage in generating physical reality in the mind. We would not be able to see things as "out there" if we did not take this step. This means that they would not be audible or visible to our five senses. When fear-based beliefs lend solidity to thought forms, they create an illusion of separation in the mind. In the human mind, fear is just love-based truth flipped upside down. Truth that is grounded in love is the blueprint, or flawless image, for our individual and social existences. Our physical reality is generated when the high frequency light of Spirit shines through the soul's blueprint for our lives and into our minds. An analogy would be that of light beaming through an eye's lens and passing through the soul's light of Spirit. The photos are upside down at first. To repair this so-called illusion, our body is designed to communicate the pictures back to Spirit via the heart. The brain receives an upside-down image from the eye, and then converts it into a right-side-up, three-dimensional physical image in the same way. Spiritual enlightenment is the process of reversing the polarity of the world and turn fear-based beliefs into love-based truths via spiritual enlightenment.

Is There Anything That We May Do to Become Spiritually Awakened?

Perceiving the illusion of separation with our body and giving that knowledge back to spirit via our heart for rectification is a process of spiritual development. Anxiety, sadness, impatience, and grief are all examples of negative emotions that the body experiences because of pictures given substance by fear-based beliefs. Having these sentiments is a sign that we are looking at things incorrectly. Our illusion of separation begins at birth and continues until the end of our lives as the most severe experience possible. Consciousness may travel through time and space before we are born and after we have died. There are no others, no out there, and no separation. These things may be conducted in our physical life experience through distant seeing and the development of our sixth sense or psychic awareness, both of which are non-physical ways of perceiving. Illusion of separation develops and strengthens during our bodily life experience. We develop a tremendous reservoir of thoughts and feelings in our minds that is outside ourselves. It is a lot like the life of a caterpillar, which eats and develops until it is as large as a caterpillar can be. We were given many choices at some time in our lives. There is a zero point in the physical heart of each of us, a point of connection to the divine source. When the illusion of separation's upside-down pictures are allowed to pass through this spiritual heart, they can be turned right side up in the mind, resulting in a physical life experience we like to refer to as heaven on Earth or nirvana.

Heaven on Earth may be experienced whenever we see anything with our bodies and allow it to be flipped over in our hearts, which gives the image solidity with love-based truth. For us to have a fulfilling and meaningful life, we must cultivate the quality of love-based truth in ourselves and others. This change and spiritual enlightenment process has been supported and encouraged by humankind throughout history. One of the most ancient methods of self-healing is meditation. Today, we can enhance our meditation experience with the use of modern technology.

It is not necessary to struggle to grow spiritually. If we believe that finding out who we really are and how we relate to God is a long and grueling process that requires us to overcome a wide range of hurdles and inconvenient situations, we miss the point. Acquire correct understanding of your true nature and God. Acquire knowledge of what to do to allow your intrinsic ability to be spiritually awake to be realized—and use it. Aspire to be totally, spiritually awake. Truth seekers often suffer from unneeded obstacles and moments of frustration and despair because they lack an intellectual knowledge of their core nature, the existence of God, what they expect to accomplish, and how to do it. They may have excellent intentions, but they are unsure of what they are doing. Subliminal desires learned cultural ideas, incoherent decisions, or the behaviors and mistaken opinions of spiritually unconscious individuals influence their thoughts and actions. They are usually faced by these tough challenges. You can learn about God from those who already know about Him. When you improve your intellect and intuition, you will discover your inner wisdom, which grows into knowledge and understanding of God.

God (from old German meaning the ultimate good) has a transcendent (beyond relative, objective phenomena) and a modified aspect with qualities. As members of a larger whole, we can experience the transcendent quality since we are a part of it. In spiritual awakening, the transformed feature can be linked to and grasped. Having spiritual insight is not a goal to be reached, and it is not the result of any cause. Realizing who we truly are and how we fit into God's plan is the first step toward making our dreams a reality. In most cases, spiritual awakening is a gradual process that begins with little insights and progresses to a fuller understanding. It is also possible for it to happen right away. Be aware of the abrupt awakening that may come while calmly, carefully adhering to your path of study and spiritual practice. To be patient is to be cool and composed while fulfilling one's obligations and pursuing worthwhile goals. To be skilled is to be able to think and act with fluency. To stick with anything is to keep going even if you do not feel like it. To learn something of value, one must engage in fruitful study. Insights can be gained through engaging in useful spiritual practices that open our minds to added information.

If you are interested in being spiritually awakened, you do not need to wait until after you die to do it. Furthermore, you should not view money in this way: as a prize for doing well. In the world, there are millions of "decent" individuals whose spiritual awareness is limited and whose desire to become more conscious is not yet overwhelming. We are all destined to achieve enlightenment and return to our natural state of consciousness at some point in our lives.

Because of its interactions with the primal field of nature, a projected vibration of its power manifests time, space, and subtle cosmic forces from which universes are generated. We were expressed as individualized units of pure consciousness. A person's awareness is obscured when he or she becomes individuated, since the person is drawn to or projected into the sphere of primal nature. The unit then attracts a fine material substance, allowing it to have a degree of intellectual discrimination as a result. More mental content is drawn to the mind's processes of perception and conceptualization. Even though these coverings are restrictive, they allow the soul to interact and function in the physical world.

The Healing Power of the Living Spirit

The reality of human existence is that a human being is a living spirit and that his or her true self is found in his or her innermost self. A person's physical body is both a vehicle and a container for the unconstrained spirit of intelligent divine power, which expresses in distinct ways through and inside it. Because of this, the body could not stand in the way of the spirit of life (the ancient Egyptians called it Ka, and the Chinese called it Chi) that is inside it. No perception of conflict can exist between the two, as they are actually one. It is just the outside and the interior of the same vessel, but they are distinct. Each is the other's complement. The only actual reality is the union of the two, or rather, the one that appears from the convergence of various intellect levels. Even being two separate entities, mind and body are the same thing manifested in many ways. Both extreme materialists and extreme idealists make the same mistake when they try to understand the relative without understanding the absolute. Trying to achieve an outside without an inside and an interior without an outside are two separate mistakes. To build a large organization, both are needed. This is what I call the Holistic Spiritual Approach (HSA).

Both the physical body, with all its glands, nerves, muscles, blood, bones, and flesh, and the intelligent power that created it for the sole purpose of manifesting through it are as real as each other. Our body is a conduit through which the universal forces of the cosmos flow. Other than that, there are a number of unique elements that can only be explained by a spiritual principle. The fact is that the life of the body and the life of the mind are similar, with the only variation between the two being the level of intellect and vibrational energy. Only a few steps beyond our usual perspective will reveal that our mental and physical lives are not separate entities, but are part of life, with no line of demarcation possible other than an arbitrary one. The body is more than just a beautiful and complex living unit governed by the divine powers of the cosmos. An inner spiritual essence, which is the source and spring of all the body's essential functions and acts, animates every atom and cell.

When it comes to the practice of healing, the above reality is neglected. When it is taken into consideration, more healing will take place. Because of this, one who fixes watches should not only focus on the hands of a chronometer but also on the springs that make it tick, as well as any other parts that may be malfunctioning. It is the intuition's ability to grasp ideas from the infinite, that greater dimension of life and intelligence that fills all space but is not clear to the physical sight, which inspires great scientific discoveries. The ideas come from a higher source and are passed on to the human mind, where they are developed into practical applications. The spirit of life may appear to be far away from us at times, but it is closer to us than our own heartbeats. Healing ourselves or others requires us to rise above the domain of symptoms and senses so that we may see things as they really are, rather than how they appear to be. Let us not forget that the goal behind my book is to help students and beginners of mental treatment programs better understand this inner domain of life. Since Jesus discovered and employed it with such tremendous success, the pool of salvation or the system of healing power has not been drained. It persists as an infinite source and fountain of eternal life and joy.

Most of us have a problem because the (pool of life) is too deep for us, and purely materialistic science lacks the tools to reach the hidden depths of this pool in search of the real meaning of life. We lack the guts to enter the intelligent life pool and allow ourselves to be repaired. As soon as a person is truly recognized, the power is always at his or her fingertips. Let us take a notable example of this great life connectedness in our human body. The vagus nerve (a major nerve responsible for the regulation of internal organ functions such as digestion, heart rate, and respiratory rate) is a tangible emblem of that power in humans that sends signals of feeling to various parts of the body to activate it. Messages from the brain, stomach, heart, lungs, and intestines all travel through the vagus nerve to these many locations in our bodies. The vagus nerve is like a telegraph line that connects all these important cell regions, or cities of cells. Because of a lack of a suitable term, we will refer to these cells as the Spiritual Prototypes, or precise activities performed by spirit to achieve desired outcomes, which together form a whole human being. According to my observations, the many systems of mental healing currently gaining scientific attention have appeared in the same sequence through which intelligent life brought the universe into being, lives in it, manifests through it, and rules it. All of this can only suggest that human nature is evolving much more on the inside.

To live a healthy life, one must help others do the same. One person's thoughts may spread like wildfire via an outbreak of sickness, such as cholera. The same principle applies to the propagation of other concepts. On May 8, 1945, V-E (Victory in Europe day) was marked. That was the day that Great Britain and the United States celebrated victory in Europe. Cities in both nations and all over the world celebrated the defeat of the Nazis. How quickly the pleasure of the earth's return to peace spread across the planet! Joy spread from mind to mind because of this. Everyone's mental condition has an impact on everyone else's since all life is a manifestation of the one great universal life.

4

Scientific Approach to Spiritual Integration in Counseling Psychology

In the last few decades, counseling psychology has gotten a lot more culturally conscious. Counselors are encouraged to recognize and respect the client's culture, sexual orientation, age, gender, and socioeconomic background as well as the client's talents, spiritual beliefs, and practices in this innovative approach to therapy. This is what makes up a client's identity, what the person is good at, and what the client needs to improve on. However, spirituality is rarely, if ever, given the attention it deserves in counseling training programs. Most graduate counseling psychology schools provide a course on religion or spirituality. Interest in incorporating spirituality into therapy has grown recently. Something has been lacking in terms of recognizing, admitting, and appreciating the significance of one's challenges. This rising need implies that this has been the case for some time. The American Counseling Association created a branch for spiritual therapy to raise awareness of the role of spirituality in counseling.

In his book "The Biology of Belief" written by B. Lipton, he stated "Spirituality is now accepted in scientific circles. Scientific circles accept the word (spirit) as much as science fundamentalist groups embrace (evolution)." There is an enormous difference in how spiritualists and scientists see life. Spiritualists turn to God, the omnipotent, benevolent, eternal, and supernatural creator, or some other intangible source of belief, when their lives are out of order. For scientists, a chemical element or source is their first line of defense when things go awry. They can only get comfort from a medication like aspirin. Many scientists have revealed that their scientific principles had led them to a spiritual revelation that they had previously considered unthinkable. Added Dr. Lipton, "The most recent breakthroughs in physics and cell research are forging new bridges between the realms of science and spirit." Because of this shift in focus away from spirit, science's original aim was rewritten from scratch.

Today's scientific endeavors are focused on dominating and controlling nature, rather than trying to understand the natural order and live in peace with it. Human civilization is on the verge of spontaneous combustion and chaotic self-destruction because of the technology that has been developed because of this worldview. Human beings are living lives without moral compasses or common higher values systems because they are drifting away from the spiritual dimension. As Dr. Lipton said, the modern society has shifted its focus from spiritual explanations of life truths to a race for material wealth. Material and physical resources are the most crucial factors in this game. How did we come to this stage in the first place? "There was a period when it was necessary for scientists to separate themselves from the domain of spirit, or at least the distortion of spiritual consciousness by the Church," Dr. Lipton said in response to this topic. If something conflicted with Church doctrine, this strong institution was engaged in stifling it.

Kardek claimed in his book "The Spirit's Book" that some individuals believe that spiritual conceptions and thoughts might upset one's mental capabilities; hence, they speak out against the practice of spiritualism and distance themselves from its ideals. He stated that it is not surprising that most people have such negative views about spirituality. He went on to say that at scientific institutes, spirituality is usually omitted from their research and talks. They believe that if spiritual conceptions are embraced, they might elicit worries and exploit vulnerable imaginations. In the same book, Kardek wrote, "All strong mental obsessions might lead to madness. Obsessive personalities may be seen in the arts, sciences, and even religion. The brain's abnormal states are at the foundation of mental disease. Defective abilities result from a defective tool (the brain)."

A biological deficiency in the brain is the major reason of a person's insanity, which results in the brain's ability to make incorrect assessments of reality. As a result, some persons engage in a variety of interests while supporting a healthy mental state, while others feel unwell because of even the tiniest amount of mental stimulation. A predisposition has the properties of a fixed thought when it exists. In the same way as someone who is obsessed with God, angels and Satan, some people with an extreme wealth, power, parenting, or political or social philosophy could be the center focus of his mind. Insane spiritism or obsessional spirituality is a very real possibility for a religious fanatic who is obsessed with spirits.

It has been centuries since the dawn of scientific discoveries, and recently the entire world has seen a constant, publicized attack on all things spiritual or religious in nature by defenders of enlightened rationalism, as explained in the book "Beyond Physicalism" by Kelly, Crabtree and Marshall. As a result, these people see themselves and contemporary mainstream science as dependable defenders of the intellectual qualities of reason and objectivity against the retreating forces of irrationality and superstition. Crabtree and Marshall further explained: "In their view, the picture depicted above is true, and to think otherwise is to renounce centuries of scientific progress, unleash the black torrent of occultism, and revert to primitive super-naturalist ideas typical of ancient times."

These advancements have led to an in-depth scientific understanding of nature and humanity that can accept spiritual truths while also refuting the useless, overblown ideas asserted by the critics of the world's great faiths. This is based on several scientific developments. There is no one religious doctrine in spirituality, although spiritual counselors prefer to remain thoroughly founded in science while widening its scope. Spiritual counselors of today are trying to discover a common road away from religious and scientific fundamentalism. Psychiatric spiritual therapy is an excellent illustration of this intermediate ground. For the treatment of human mental and psychological disorders, we rely on spiritual and metaphysical applications. Our spiritual counselors use psychokinesis (PK) as an excellent illustration of the latest scientific ideas that we employ in our counseling programs. Kelly, Crabtree and Marshall described psychokinesis in their book "Beyond Physicalism" as the power of a personality to affect the movement of physical and biological things without the need of bodily exertion. To put it another way, it shows that our thoughts have real-world consequences. Scientifically, it might be categorized as a severe psychological effect. In PK, mind over matter may be proved in a very forceful and unambiguous way. To answer the topic of PK, we must also answer the question of how we can control our own bodies.

In their book "Beyond Physicalism", Kelly, Crabtree and Marshall explain more about the metaphysical effect on the physical material: "The new cosmological vision of the world that we live in transforms the entire physical world or what we call the real world perceived by humans into a small part of a much vaster world called the astral world, which spans everything imaginable, including worlds vastly different from our physical world and, probably countless other physical worlds as well." This is seen as a major shift in modern philosophy, which has tended to perceive physical matter as the ultimate reality, and to understand dreams and other extrasomatic experiences as products of physical matter. There is a whole new way of thinking about our shared memories of non-somatic events, what Weiss dubbed "the real world," which is vastly different from the way we have previously thought about it (the vital world). He said that the concept of trans-physical realms is opposed to the current prevalent theory of materialism and is hence routinely dismissed in academic circles. Kelly, Crabtree and Marshall added: "It should be noted that our civilization is the only one in history to have rejected the existence of these worlds for around the last three hundred years." In our society, we are taught from an early age that the non-physical aspects of our experience are just pure imagination.

New generations of spiritual counselors play a vital role in educating their clients about scientific notions like mind over matter, the psychokinesis theory, and trans-physical realms that underpin their counseling programs. As said by McMinn in his book "Psychology, Theology and Spirituality", "Spiritual counselors fulfill three functions concurrently. Primarily, they are fully involved in the interpersonal exchanges that take place during therapy sessions. Counselors are watchers who pay attention to what is going on in the relationship, as well as what is working and what is not. Lastly, they are spiritual engineers of the counseling relationship, changing the connection by becoming more empathetic when a client feels isolated, more distant when a client becomes overly reliant, and enforcing proper boundaries throughout the counseling relationship. Developing a trusting relationship with their clients is an essential element of their treatment."

Based on this new generation of modern counseling psychology and mental health, several counseling organizations, such as the American Counseling Association (ACA), the Association for Spiritual, Ethical and Religious Values in Counseling (ASERViC), and the Council for Accreditation of Counseling and Related Educational Programs (CACREP), are stepping up their efforts to incorporate spirituality into the counseling process. Recognition of the importance and usefulness of discussing spirituality with customers confirms its validity and significance. A person's spiritual beliefs should be included in treatment as they are incorporated into the individual's life. It is a person's unique belief system that helps him or her build and sustain a healthy mental and physical well-being when properly integrated. It also provides individuals with a sense of purpose, optimism, and perseverance when they experience adversity. The spirituality of a person might help the person link the loose ends of his or her life story. When it comes to interpersonal connections, however, a client's religious or spiritual convictions might have a significant impact on how he or she wants to be treated. As a result, clients will be able to understand how they can sustain themselves, accept responsibility for themselves and their own decisions, and therefore reach congruence and integrity. To ignore the role of spiritual forces in shaping and creating human relationships, as well as the meaning and purpose of one's life, is unfortunately to miss the very essence of what it is to be human. A profession based on empathy and forging an authentic, therapeutic relationship may require opening whatever religious or spiritual literature the client brings. In recent years, and according to Miller and Rollnick, most people in the United States have identified with some form of religious belief, even if they are not active participants in a particular religion, and their beliefs have a profound impact on their worldviews, relationships, self-concepts, and problems.

5

The Spiritual Factor in Mental Health Programs

As a result of the ideas of Maslow, "transpersonal psychology," which emphasizes the individual's existential need to be "transcendental and metaphysical" in aspects of religion and spirituality, and which aims to synthesize Eastern and Western science, appeared as the first serious approach to spirituality in modern psychology according to Gray and Bjorklund (2014). Pastoral counseling, spiritual humanistic psychology, as well as C.G.Young's "Sufi psychology/ mysticism psychology," which has a deep spiritual base in the eastern part of the world, are all examples of hypothetic backgrounds for religious and spiritual approaches. While traditional Christian and Eastern (such as meditation and yoga) tools, like prayer and holy book interpretation, are still used in spiritual psychological counseling, new schools of religious and spiritual psychotherapy are also springing up all over the world.

Using spiritual counseling approaches appropriately in clinics can have a significant impact on the mental health and well-being of patients, according to McMinn (2011). Moral codes and application guidelines that highlight the necessity of respecting religious and spiritual differences are also produced. Psychiatrists have found spirituality-based therapies to be useful. Spiritual therapies have been shown to be more successful than secular ones. There are a lot of mental strategies based on religious and spiritual resources that have been used by many practitioners in the last ten years. In these strategies, spirituality is one of the methods employed for mental rehabilitation and problem-solving. Psychiatrists are urged to look at more than one issue when assessing their patients' mental health. Acknowledging and respecting clients' spirituality is regarded as one of the qualities that contribute to the success of treatment and bring the therapist and client together.

While collaborating with people to help them unleash their greatest forms of awareness and connect with the infinite higher inventive mind, spiritual counselors and healers focus on improving their clients' abilities to heal themselves and their relationships. That does not imply directly influencing the patient's mental process; rather it is an indirect manner of rewiring and redirecting the patient's awareness toward the spiritual path. Spiritual counseling serves as a means to keep the counselor's own thoughts and beliefs separate from the patient's beliefs, convince the counselor of the truth about the patient (which is one of the main core manifestations of the infinite) and ensure that infinite consciousness and the patient's own consciousness can be united in a positive higher mind union that is unique in nature.

The counselor's whole spiritual therapy procedure is a self-directed effort to address the client's erroneous belief. The counselor must be able to plainly perceive this. The spiritual counselor is aware that the tangible manifestations of his or her misguided views include poverty, disease, and other adversity. They are his or her primary focus. In spiritual therapy, one of the most important principles is that the counselor perceives the human body not as flesh and bones, but as spiritual substance, whose shape may be altered just as readily. The spiritual counselor can support his or her belief in the physical's potential to change because of this awareness. The therapeutic power of counseling is perfect when the counselor's belief about the client is obvious, without any doubt or mental reservations.

Do You Know What to Expect in a Typical Session of Spiritual Counseling?

Although there is no standard approach for a session of spiritual therapy, each counselor's views and procedures will influence the process. During the session, you can expect to get spiritual direction. Every counselor is unique, so if you are not happy with your current one, you can always find a new one. Even if you talk to someone who has had a positive experience with a spiritual counselor, this does not mean that yours will be the same. Before devising a plan of action to help you in your time of need, your counselor or therapist should listen to you and completely understand your situation. Your choice of counselor will also differ depending on the modalities of therapy the counselor uses and how his or her personality affects the treatment you will be receiving. There are a number of things you need to keep in mind while looking for a spiritual counselor, including whether the counselor is non-denominational or denominational.

People's spiritual or religious views can aid in the therapeutic healing process. Both psychotherapists and spiritual counselors use evidence-based methods and therapies to aid clients. Future studies are still needed to implement evidence-based spiritual counseling programs. Based on my many tears of experience as a spiritual counselor, I did observe a positive impact on emotional and psychological well-being on patients if they are encouraged to include their faith and spirituality into therapy. Individuals should not be held to a higher standard because of where they find relief. For example, during the mourning process following the death of a loved one, spiritual counselling can be beneficial. For some, the loss of loved ones might lead them to reassess their spiritual or religious views. Anxiety caused by a lack of meaning or spiritual guidance can also be alleviated by using certain types of mindful spiritual meditation. Overall, you should only seek spiritual therapy from someone who is professionally trained, certified, and licensed and/or registered, who can provide you with the treatment you require, rather than seek spiritual counsel in general.

Consequently, spiritual counseling's therapeutic impact stems from the practitioner's thoughts, which are manifested in the client. This kind of projected contact with the infinite, which is referred to as mental happiness, can be achieved through a spiritual approach to therapy, which sets up a practical relationship with the infinite. For the sake of humanity, this is a sensible strategy. Frederic Bailes, in his book "Basic Principles of the Mind", described how infinite dimensions have existed throughout human history. He said, "Theologians throughout the centuries have resolutely grappled with the question of the essence of God. But their efforts have gone from primordial man's rudimentary notions to the strict dogmas of the Dark and Middle Ages, to more enlightened concepts of modern humans, on the boundless higher awareness or heavenly holy spirit/God." Bailes asked this question in the same book: "Is God a person or a non-person?" He thought God was a mix of the two. God is spirit, mind, and body, according to him. All three existed from the beginning, except for body, which was only existent as the universe's primary unformed substance. No one of the three handled the creation of the others. This three-phase intelligence, which we label God, is difficult to define, according to Dr. Bailes, since it encompasses all that is visible and invisible.

A human body, based on these views, is an extension of God's unformed nature. God is the Divine Mind, and we are his extensions. God's Spirit is manifested in us as our spirits. The three-sided infinite connects all aspects of human existence. In the relative, humans express what God is in the perfect absolute inadequately. Spiritual counselors must thus highlight both the personal and the impersonal aspects of this relationship with God. There has been an increase in the sort of unity that exists between our clients and God. In this case, the well-known principle that like attracts like is at work. That which is harmonious tends to unite with that which is harmonious. A tight working relationship between the infinite and our thoughts is developed because of this clearing of earthiness in our thoughts. You cannot have the correct relationship with God's creative law of life, which appears from the pure essence of love, if you are full of hatred and prejudice. That which does not dread is not in harmony with the fearful. It is not necessary for most of our clients to be perfectly free of their mental issues, but we as spiritual counselors can help them let go of the inappropriate negative, deforming thought patterns if they wish to enter this connection that precedes the healing of their souls. We, as spiritual counselors, should be always ready to help our clients in their journey to enlightenment. Even though they have human flaws, we may assist them in re-creating God's nature by employing the creative process.

Dr. Herbert Benson said in his book "The Relaxation Effect" that "physiologic modifications of the relaxation response are related with what has been called an altered state of consciousness" because of our work with patients to help them grow spiritually. In recent years, the phrase "altered state of consciousness" has been more widely accepted. Ecstasy, selflessness, quiet tranquility, or a synthesis of all these sentiments have all been described by those who have experienced altered states of consciousness. As spiritual counselors, we employ meditation as a primary means of achieving a changed state of consciousness. Some people find the term meditation difficult to understand because it conjures images of Eastern cults or Christian monks who spend most of their waking hours in their cells pondering God, according to Dr. Benson. As spiritual counselors, it is our duty to help our clients in their quest for enlightenment by using components from a variety of meditation practices. The process of resolving inner incompleteness and minimizing inner conflict is a universal psychological process, not only one related to religion. Through prayer, you are always reminded of your spirit, and there is no greater source of power in your life than becoming quiet, being silent, and understanding what actual power prayer is. It is safe to say that prayer is both the oldest and most widespread spiritual activity in the United States. Most major faiths see it as an essential part of spirituality. "All faiths are real," argues George Lucas, whose blockbuster *Star Wars* films play on religious concepts like good and evil. "Religion is simply a container for faith," he concludes. What keeps us calm and balanced, though, is our faith in God. Prayer's effectiveness may be based on the release of mental and emotional tension, as well as a sense of connection to a higher power. Another effective tool of connecting with the infinite is reading sacred words from the heart. In every global religion, there is a set of sacred books. The 'Koran" was Muhammad Ali's "spiritual, guiding book," as he always said. The last effective tool is connecting with nature. We have all been in awe of Earth's beauty at some point in our lives, and this is a tremendously spiritual moment.

Spiritual counseling employs a number of common methods. Because it includes the unique philosophic cognitive processes, sentiments, and behaviors of everyone, spirituality is not limited to a specific religious philosophy. To help you decide your purpose in life, this might be a valuable resource. Denominational counselors may include their own religious rituals and traditions into counselling. For example, your therapy may include some time spent in prayer. Practicing forgiveness or drawing on the guidance found in the Bible may also be part of this form of treatment. Counselors who are not affiliated with a particular religious tradition may take inspiration from other forms of spirituality, such as meditation, yoga, or relaxation methods. To summarize the spiritual counseling primary therapeutic instruments, they are as follows.

Prayer

Praying allows us to reinterpret and acknowledge the events and circumstances in our lives, which is why it is considered a cognitive coping strategy. Individuals of many faiths pray, even some who have abandoned their faith and adopted a more logical lifestyle. People use prayer to express their feelings, desires, and needs. Spirituality is a human emotion that can only be experienced by those who are human. It is a desire to connect with the divine and feel like you are part of something sacred. This sensation is widely acknowledged for its significance and for its ability to provide a unique window into the nature of humanity. Praying as a well-known mental and spiritual rehabilitation has been around for a long time, but it has only recently been an issue for scientific study.

Prayer can be used as an icebreaker by a spiritual counselor to build a therapeutic alliance. There are many benefits to prayer, but the most significant is knowing that you are not alone. Those who pray are less worried about the future, do not see life with pessimism, and are optimistic for the future. A client's support for prospective prayer-related therapies might be helpful in this situation. A variety of thinking strategies, such as analysis of circumstances, cognitive conversation, and connective concepts, are provided to clients because of this. Contemplating an incident or scenario and totally dedicating oneself to it with the support of prayer helps the client acquire insight into his or her own difficulties and accomplishes reconstruction in this setting. Having a group of people pray for you might help you feel less alone and more optimistic about your recovery.

Patience

Patience, in this context, refers to the ability to persevere in the face of adversity, such as the death of a loved one. Patience means enduring, resisting, opposing, and dealing to overcome pain, suffering, and difficulties. Patience develops maturity by allowing a person to achieve and defend his or her goals. If you do not deviate from the path, you will be able to save power for the future.

Submission

As a result of one's faith in God and one's belief in fate, submission is inevitable. Another religious approach to dealing with inconvenient situations is to submit to them. Grace is available to those who have experienced hardships in their lives. When one finds someone in a worse circumstance than oneself, one is more likely to show grace. Submissive people are more powerful than those who do not believe in it. Because they are immune to the struggles of life, they do not feel disturbed by them. Outsiders have no way of knowing that you have submitted. A person's inner world is shaped by it. When faced with adversity and stress, it may be argued that submitting has a significant impact. After accomplishing what is needed, one surrenders to the will of God or the higher divine power that controls the whole universe. In this way, it creates a powerful and optimistic mindset. When dealing with clients' issues, it might be helpful to adopt this mindset. After discussing the cognitive aspects of submitting, the therapist asks the client to write down any submission moments he or she has until the next session. During the next visit, the client's favorable reactions to these instances would be assessed.

Self-Forgiveness and Forgiving Others

Clients' spiritual and religious beliefs are tapped into in the forgiving approach to help them forgive themselves and others in the process. Forgiveness is an important part of many cultures, and some individuals feel closer to the gods when they do it. Religion and spirituality exhort people to be kind, forgiving, appreciative, and thankful. There are many benefits of forgiveness. Anger, animosity, and grief can be alleviated via forgiveness. Based on my years of spiritual counseling, I found spiritual persons more cheerful, active, and friendly with others. There is a strong connection between forgiveness and spirituality for many individuals, even though forgiveness is a personal idea or concept. What questions may a spiritual counselor ask clients? "Is forgiving suitable for your religion/ spiritual values?" and "Is this suitable for your religion/spiritual values?" are two examples. An important aspect of therapy is the discussion of the need to forgive oneself.

How to Interpret Your Spiritual Dreams

It is widely accepted that dreams are the primary vehicle for one's unconscious responses to one's psychological difficulties. Dreams are the first place to begin in spiritually focused psychotherapy. According to C. G. Jung's spiritually centered dream interpretation approach in his book "The undiscovered Self," the infinite variety of dreams that include sights, symbols, and writings is what clients aim for in their interpretations of their dreams. There is a lot of talk about dream interpretation in religious texts. The interpretation of dreams in a favorable light might be a comforting factor for patients. Having dreams is a normal aspect of life. Dreams and nightmares are common for those who are experiencing difficulties, and they need to be interpreted to help the person feel better. Using dream interpretation as a spiritual therapy tool is possible. To be able to decipher dreams, one must have a good grasp of the subject matter at hand. Encouraging clients to interpret their dreams in this way is the most crucial part of dream interpretation.

Hymns and Religious Chanting

The universal attraction of music is undeniable. Sharing inner tranquility and inner tension and helping to maintain inner equilibrium are its primary functions. To put it in another way, the personal function of music helps individuals overcome emotional difficulties and create good feelings rather than negative ones by training and improving emotions associated with anger, grief, and so forth. With drug-addicted patients, music therapy had a positive influence on their anxiety, sadness, and physical activities. Music may also have both beneficial and harmful effects on humans, according to researchers who conducted a series of studies. These studies revealed that music can have a positive effect on people's mental health. For this reason, we should encourage our kids to listen to music, and promote and guide them toward music that has a positive impact on their anger and mental health. A hymn, a sort of music, is regarded to be beneficial to the clients in dealing with stress in this situation.

◆ 6 ◆

The Future of Spiritual Counseling Psychology

In the history of humans' attempts to understand themselves and their environments and to control their own fates, there is one big missing gap that remains the missing puzzle piece in knowing the truth about their existence. The constant question for a human being is whether or no he or she has an immortal spirit which belongs to the infinite dimension, and whether his or her own personal concept involves any element which can survive bodily death. Frederic Myers explained in his book "Human Personality and its Survival of Bodily Death" that "The method which our race has found most effective in acquiring knowledge is by this time familiar to all men. It is the method of modern science, that process which consists in an interrogation of nature and human existence entirely dispassionate, patient, systematic; such careful experiment and cumulative record as can often elicit from its slightest indications its deepest truths. That method is now dominant throughout the civilized world; and although in many directions' experiments may be difficult and dubious, facts rare and elusive, science works slowly, refusing to fall back upon tradition or to lunch into speculation, merely because strait is the gate which leads to valid discovery, indisputable truth. This method has never yet been applied to the important problem of the existence, the powers, the destiny of the human soul."

It is my goal in the present book to emphasize the spiritual aspect of our existence as human beings. This aspect is the conscious self of each of us—the empirical, the supraliminal self, as Meyers called it. As Meyers explains, "This conscious self does not comprise the whole of the consciousness or of the faculty within us. There exists a more comprehensive consciousness, a profounder faculty, which is still potential only as far as regards the life of earth, but from which the consciousness and the faculty of earth-life are mere selections, and which reasserts itself in its plenitude after liberating change of death. This level of spiritual consciousness of a human being forms the main front that we as spiritual counselors work on in our counseling and mental health programs."

Psychologically speaking, effective spiritual counselors can fully take part in a therapeutic relationship while stepping outside this relationship simultaneously to view the problems of the client and the nature of the counseling relationship more objectively. Counselors can also continue evaluating from outside the counseling relationship by noticing and noting the voice tone, all nonverbal gestures, and facial expressions. Mastering this effective type of psychological awareness requires extensive training, deep cultural sensitivity, and constant, supervised guided experience. There is more than all of these. Effective spiritual counselors also consider spiritual dimensions while engaging at the same time in the basic psychological elements of counseling. Connection with the infinite, understanding the real meaning of human existence, understand the concept of infinite divine love of God, and applying the rules of law of attraction in attracting more of the divine love, are all considered essential components of effective spiritual counseling.

Spiritual counseling should always involve a deep understanding of the nature of the spiritual life of the client, in order to discover how the client's problems are related to his or her spiritual level of development. Spiritual counselors need to find out if the problem is simply a behavioral habit to be eliminated or changed, or if the problem is a sign of deep, inner fears of connecting with God and others. McMinn explains these concepts further: "How can a treatment relationship be crafted to foster qualities of humility and insight? When, if ever, should prayer or scripture memory be used in counseling or prescribed to a client? Training for spiritual sensitivity may begin in the classroom or by reading spiritual classics, but it must continue in the private lives of counselors. The spiritual counselors help us understand God's grace and our own fallenness and give us opportunities to glean fragments of wisdom from our omniscient God."

Dr. Irvin Yalom, the great psychiatry scholar and professor of psychiatry at Stanford University, predicted in his book "The Gift of Therapy" the major changes in the fields of psychiatry and psychology related to the integration of the spiritual dimension in the psychiatric therapy programs: "In the future, and due to the huge economic pressures on the health care system as a whole specially on mental health counseling and psychotherapy, a cohort of therapists coming from a variety of educational disciplines (psychology, counseling, social work, pastoral counseling, clinical philosophy) will continue to pursue rigorous postgraduate training and, even in the crush of HMO and managed care reality, will find patients desiring extensive growth and change willing to make an open-ended commitment to therapy." Jeffery Kluger discussed the importance of mental health care in his study published in the special *Time* magazine edition about mental health. According to Kluger, "Statistics showed recently 450 million people world-wide suffer from some mental-health condition at any given moment, according to the WHO (World Health Organization). In the U.S. just under 1 in 5 adults will experience mental illness in a year, with anxiety disorders the most common among them. Over 21% of children ages 13 to 18 suffer from a serious mental-health condition at some point in that delicate developmental window; even among kids ages 8 to 15, the number is 13%."

The social cost of mental illness, as he confirmed, is astronomical; about 20 percent of state prisoners are thought to have a serious mental health disorder and an astonishing 70 percent of children in the juvenile justice system suffer from at least one such condition. The dollar cost of so much illness is just as terrible. "World-wide, more than $2.5 trillion per year is spent on mental-health care, a figure that's on track to hit $6 trillion by 2030, based on the latest statistics published by the National Institute of Mental Health," Kluger stated in his study. I fully agree with him; the science of psychology is still as imperfect and sublime as all the other healing arts. We journeyed an exceptionally long way to get here, from profound ignorance to crude understanding to true science that is yielding true therapies and remedies. Spiritual counseling or therapy is one of the most promising therapies that can be amazingly effective in empowering mental health therapies programs. Spiritual counseling is remarkably similar in a lot of ways to existential psychotherapy, the branch of psychology that deals with the question of human existence. This branch of psychotherapy is a very dynamic kind of therapy which faces the questions about the individual's existence.

Spiritual counseling is a form of dynamic psychotherapy. Dr Yalom defined the psychodynamics of an individual in his book "Existential Psychotherapy" as "the various unconscious and conscious forces, motives, and fears that operate within him or her. Based on this definition, spiritual counseling and therapy is one of the dynamic psychotherapies since it is based upon this dynamic model of mental functioning." Most of the programs we use for therapy in psychiatric and psychology departments are based on mental health and have always assumed that mental health can be separated from the spiritual life, an assumption that most spiritual counselors reject. There is a great need for an innovative and effective therapeutic program for spiritual growth. This suggested program must be based on our morals and values, on anthropology and theology, must focus on the spiritual teachings in scripture and religions, and must remain relevant to the various mental health problems we face. This projected program needs to be an applicable program that a regular practitioner and client can easily understand, not a complex one that can only be understood by philosophers and theologians and cannot be used in the counseling office. Most counselors and psychologists do not want to replace their mainstream commitments to behavioral, cognitive, psychodynamic, family, and other forms of therapy. However, as spiritual counselors, we need a deeper understanding of the spiritual element of wisdom in order to see ourselves, our clients, and our counseling relationships in a deeper, more spiritual way.

As McMinn explained in his book "Psychology, Theology, and Spirituality", "The fruit of the spirit described by Paul in the Gospel do not correspond perfectly with the characteristics of emotional health described by Maslow. And emotional health is different from spiritual wellbeing. However, we see substantial overlap. The more accurately we understand ourselves, the more freedom we have for emotional and spiritual health." The spiritual nature of health can be defined by the existence of the relationship between a human being and the divine. This divine concept can be the Holy Spirit, God, Allah, the higher wisdom, or the intelligent universal mind. Mental health also requires an ability to start and maintain intimate relationships. This is not saying that relationships are a sign of health. Many counseling clients have a basic ability to form and keep relationships, but usually face wrong learning patterns or difficult life circumstances; the more they develop and learn a pattern self-efficacy, their ability to maintain sound relationships and their learning patterns will improve. Based on these changes, they will be able to experience even greater freedom for healthy, positive, relationships.

Dr. McMinn discussed in detail the ideal therapeutic relationship between the spiritual counselor and the client in the same book, stating that "In some forms of counseling, the therapeutic relationship is the prototype of a healthy relationship. Some clients have rarely experienced a confiding, intimate relationship with good boundaries until they come for counseling. They learn about trust, respect, care, and empathy by seeing and interacting with the counselor. In this sense, a good spiritual counselor is a minister of God's grace, even to those who know nothing of a gracious God." A notable example of spiritual counseling's success is the AA (Alcoholics Anonymous) programs. As we all know, this great program is a global, community-based program created to help those struggling with alcohol addiction and problematic drinking to recover and get sober with the support of their families and peers and through daily meetings and discussions. During the recovery journey in this program, there are people at many distinct stages of recovery, and each stage is equally valid and important. What is clear from talking to people and listening to their stories of recovery is that those who are making the most progress and finding the most freedom from their codependency are those who work the steps and allow the steps of the program to work in their lives.

Melody Beattie stated in her book "Codependent's Guide to the Twelve Steps" that "Regardless of their progress or how much time these people have spent in the program, most have begun to have a spiritual awakening. To some, this means connecting with friends and beginning to feel and express feelings. To others, it means the power to begin taking care of themselves, despite what another person is or is not doing. To most, it means an awakening to God, an awakening to self, to who we are, to our spirits." Recent studies presented by Kluger in his book "Understanding Our Own Mind / Mental Health, a New Understanding" revealed that a sizable percentage of our physical troubles are mental in their origin, and that all physical illnesses have either a direct or indirect form of relationship to mental processes. Based on these facts, it is vital that we understand and appreciate the work of the sincere metaphysicians and spiritual counselors. That does not mean that the general psychologist can take the place of the metaphysician or spiritual counselor. A full, complete healing of the body without an adjustment of mental and emotional states will be always insufficient; therefore, it is imperative that the adjusting and healing of mental and emotional states must be accompanied by applying spiritual values.

Holmes explained this concept in his book "Living the Science of Mind": "In the early days of spiritual therapeutics it was believed that a practitioner could not successfully treat patients if a physician was attending them, or if they were using material methods for relief. Now we know that this was based on superstition. We no longer give it any serious thought. The metaphysician and the spiritual counselor feel it a privilege to be called into consultation with a physician or with a psychologist. He has learned to appreciate the fields of medicine and surgery." Our patients' religious and spiritual beliefs are significant to them. Existential concerns may be at the root of many of their difficulties. Spirituality and religious activities should so be incorporated into our therapy plan. The Bio-Psycho-Social-Spiritual concept (BPSS) must be incorporated into our psychiatric and mental health practices. When it comes to the topic of religion and mental health, I suggest that spirituality and religious activities should be taken into consideration while writing a psychiatric history for patients. We often inquire about a patient's denomination during a mental history. We are usually not interested in finding out how the patient's religious beliefs affect him or her. For patients, we should ask what religion and spirituality signifies in their lives. Medical records should include information about religious upbringing and experiences, as well as how religion has helped the patient cope with life's challenges. What religious encounters has the patient had in the past that were negative? What kind of spiritual and social assistance has the patient received from his church, synagogue, mosque, or temple? How much involvement does he or she have in the religious institution that he or she belongs to? The recommended therapy may contradict with some religious views. It is common for some religious organizations to oppose any medical treatment. The current mental condition of some patients may be worsened by religious disputes and frustrations. Religious personnel who perpetrate sexual assault, other terrible occurrences that lead patients to abandon their religious practices, and unanswered prayers are only a few examples. It is possible to take a history of spirituality and religious experiences with the help of questionnaires. Discussing spiritual and religious experiences with the patient will help build a stronger therapeutic bond. The counselor's own progress might potentially be reversed because of this.

Patients' religious beliefs should be respected and supported if they help them cope better and do not harm their mental health. Because fasting and prayer might help a patient cope better, these practices should be promoted. To improve mental health, we need to confront some of the assumptions that might harm us. This must be managed delicately. We should wait until we have a clear understanding of the patient and the challenges at hand before deciding on a course of action. Patients may want to talk about their subjective experiences and existential demands with their therapists. Listening to them is a worthwhile investment of time. We can benefit from cooperation with religious leaders in this area. A cooperation between psychiatry and faith-based groups is critical. Many communities in the United States still support a prominent role for clergy, and the value of clergy in the treatment of those with mental health issues is rising according to McMinn (2011). For them, it is critical to examine the relationship between the mental health team and faith-based organizations. There must be a cooperation between mental health practitioners and religious leaders for this relationship to be successful.

Despite the rising amount of research on religion and spirituality in the counseling psychology field, there are still numerous topics that need future investigation. Religious and spirituality research has been hindered by the belief that religion and spirituality cannot be examined scientifically. Spiritual counselors should confront these misconceptions. In the face of these misconceptions, researchers will continue to examine religion and spirituality objectively. My suggestion is that studies on spirituality and religion should be expanded beyond the United States, where most studies have focused. Future studies should include more diverse populations. It is time for researchers to include more non-Christian religions in their studies. Counselors should always broaden their knowledge of world religions and become more literate when confronted with clients of many religious persuasions.

To better understand their clients' worldviews, counselors might build consultation connections with spiritual or religious leaders and utilize them as resources to feel more comfortable addressing these ideas in counseling. Researchers and doctors need to agree on the concepts of spirituality and religion. Experts in the field of spiritual psychology have urged scientists to investigate the influence of religion and spirituality on a wide range of issues, such as mental illness, addictions, and physical health. Most of these relationships have concentrated on the good influence that religion has had on many aspects of clients' lives, and more attention should be paid to the possible disadvantages of religion.

Counselor education programs should take advantage of the growing body of research on religion. If religious and spiritual topics are addressed more often in therapy sessions, counselors will feel more secure in their abilities to do so. There are both positive and bad aspects to religious and/or spiritual instruction for counselors in the current scenario. There is a lack of formal training in religious or spiritual concerns in counselor education programs. Religion and spirituality are rarely viewed as a diversity issue. Faculty members in counselor training programs rarely consider religious or spiritual traditions to be significant to students. Religion and spirituality were not the primary emphases of many courses; instead, they were offered as subtopics in larger courses. It was common for programs to have holes in their curriculum, omitting critical issues like the connection between religion and mental health. The possibility of future counselors to include religion and spirituality in their work was recently recognized by Ponder in his book: "The Dynamic Laws of Prayers". In most counseling courses, students should have the opportunity to talk or write about their spiritual or religious experiences.

◆ 7 ◆

Spirituality and Modern Psychology

Spiritual psychology, as I previously mentioned, has been around for a long time, but only recently has it become a distinct area of psychology. A group of pioneering psychologists, including William James, Carl Jung, Roberto Assagioli, and Abraham Maslow, introduced the concept of spiritual and transcendental psychology. In 1969, Abraham Maslow and others published the first issue of the *Journal of Transpersonal Psychology*, which has since become the main academic journal in the area. This journal focuses on how the mind works from a spiritual perspective, while it also enhances our understanding of how psychology and mental health can be enhanced by conducting spiritual psychology discussions and research.

Academic institutions are not the only places where spiritual psychologists are employed. Many people are self-employed entrepreneurs, life coaches, professional speakers, and authors, among other things. Those who study transpersonal psychology have a deeper understanding of themselves and the myriad human situations they encounter, which often inspires them to pursue careers in the field. Understanding the self to this level has a profound effect on those who have experienced it, and they feel a need to share this information with others.

While researching the spiritual role in counseling psychology through my doctoral research, I gained a better knowledge of how important the spiritual factor in transpersonal psychology is, especially after identifying the basic therapeutic elements that were the core of the spiritual integration concept in counseling psychology programs. In this cosmos we dwell in, all of us and all our fellow creatures, are anchored in the mind of God or what we call the higher mind. Humans did not want it this way, yet we must accept the fact that this is the way things are. Everywhere we go, there will always be a greater power that will exceed and overcome our human limited power; at the same time, the holy divine life power will always be present in us. For this reason, learning to tune into the mind of God, or the higher mind part of our psyche, will help us to connect with the core source of good positive vibrations. We are tuning into the most dynamic infinite higher mind of reality in all space and time if we do that. To assist individuals overcome their fear of talking to God or the higher mind, spiritual counseling is one of the most powerful therapeutic techniques. It teaches people that God or the higher mind speaks a whole other language, a positive language of love, and that there is nothing negative about it.

Tuning into the higher mind part of our psyche, the divine godly dimension, can be applied through affirmative meditation. Affirmative meditation is a powerful method for linking the human soul to the divine Spirit by employing the great spiritual healing instrument of prayers. Spiritual counselors can utilize their therapeutic intimacy (or what is called therapeutic alliance) with their clients to open their conscious mind to the process of communicating with their higher mind/God and preparing their clients to receive God's replies. "God never deserts us, and we shall never have to convince God to be good," wrote Holmes in his book "Living the Science of Mind." To see the miracle take place, all we need to do is to change our whole mental and spiritual view on life.

Mental healing cannot be fully grasped or appreciated unless the spiritual counselor studying it really puts it into action. We should all strive to become practitioners, even if we only have ourselves as patients. That is the most important thing. Conscious and purposeful usage is like any other natural law. Because only thought can get to that which is the product of thought, a spiritual counselor focuses on thoughts while collaborating with clients. "We do not anticipate thought to achieve some physical condition independent of mind," Holmes said in the same book: "Assuming that all form is a manifestation of thought and mind regulates its manifestation, mental healing must be founded on this presupposition."

Thoughts and concepts should be broken down into simple ideas by a good spiritual counselor, who then continues to disentangle the incorrect and inappropriate blocking concepts by recognizing the omnipresence of truth, or God. Because the mind can never work independently of consciousness, an inexperienced practitioner who treats sickness or circumstances as if they were separate from consciousness will quickly learn that he or she is inadvertently trying to inflict harm from outside. He or she is trying to direct the mind to something that is not mental, or to direct thinking to something that does not exist in the mental realm. He or she is on the verge of oblivion. As soon as a spiritual counselor learns that everything is either absolute mind or mind in a tangible form, it becomes easier for him or her to shift his or her thoughts in a good direction. A spiritual mind counselor does just this. He or she does this on purpose and with full awareness. A person's belief in the curability or incurability of a sickness, the length of time it will take to heal, and the likelihood that it will take to cure is everything that a person's mental illness or disease shows to him or her. Since every mental illness is a negative statement in one's mind from the perspective of spiritual counseling, it is impossible for a spiritual counselor to treat one ailment as biological and another as mental.

Spiritual counselors tell their clients that if God is present in and around them, and if they are connected to their divine higher mind, there is nothing to fear since absolute pure love throws out fear. This fear cannot exist where love is constantly present. Fear has no place in the spiritual counselor's office or in the presence of anybody else. As a human being, you are initially a spiritual being; thus, you should not dread anything working through you that may lead to death, because there is no such thing as death in this world based on universal spiritual teachings. Regardless of the fact that we are dealing with unseen (spiritual) forces, they are no less real than any other power of nature. It is impossible to see anything spiritual in the world. In mainstream psychology, the principle of mind is unseen, and its practice is invisible, but its effects are the word made manifest. For this reason, it is important to assess our positions in relation to the present approach to mental research and establish where we agree and where we differ from the present psychological and therapeutic techniques.

A growing amount of scientific evidence supports spirituality's health advantages according to Holmes (2005). Spirituality and Healing in Medicine is a course offered by the Harvard Medical School Continuing Education Department. It brings together religious academics and medical professionals from across the world to examine how spirituality might be used to alleviate sickness and pain. Since it began in 2011, the course has been taught by Herbert Benson, MD, chief of Beth Israel Deaconess Medical Center's Division of Behavioral Medicine and has attracted 1,000 doctors and other health care professionals from throughout the country and across the world. About sixty medical schools now offer comparable classes, up from three medical schools only five years ago, according to Kluger (2019) and the academics who teach the courses. According to Lipton (2016), surveys of 269 family doctors in 1996 found that 99 percent of them believed that prayer, meditation, or other spiritual and religious practices can be helpful in medical treatment; more than half of them said they currently incorporate relaxation or meditation techniques into the treatment of patients. Herbert Benson's study has shown that regular meditation (a type of spiritual technique) can reduce stress and improve relaxation and general well-being, since chronic stress is severely damaging to the body.

Spirituality and Existentialism

Religion and spirituality have a long and historic connection with existential ideas. This connection has become a growing specialty in the field of psychology called existential psychology. However, existentialism has been misunderstood for many years as hostile to religion and the belief in God because of its roots in Soren Kierkegaard's Christian theology according to McMinn (2011). In response, critics point out that many later existentialist thinkers were atheists and agnostics. Many important philosophical and psychological theories share this sentiment; thus, it does not make the existential school of thinking unique. Friedrich Nietzsche and Jean-Paul Sartre, two of the most influential thinkers of the twentieth century, were both atheists. Despite this, there is a widespread belief that existentialism is a religion. A statement about the history of existential thinking is made by the fact that such conflicting mistakes are made in understanding the fundamental essence of its history and the structure of its ideas. An existential viewpoint on religion requires a thorough comprehension of the most prevalent misconceptions. Most established theoretical viewpoints are not static or unified, and existential psychology is no exception.

Psychology of Existence

There are two main schools of thought in existential psychology, and it is crucial to emphasize this. One view is referred to as the non-spiritual approach while the other is the spiritual approach. In non-spiritual existentialism, there are no answers to the questions we have about our own existence. Atheism is a tenet of this concept of human life. In contrast, the spiritual perspective sees an element of awe in human experience and connects it to some form of transcendence, or spiritual, response to the existential issues. This, however, does not necessarily advocate the presence of God. Followers of the spiritual existentialism contend that there are no solutions to these problems in the non-spiritual school of thought.

As a spiritual existentialist counselor, I would describe myself as awe-inspiring in the middle of my worst doubts. Without religion or understanding, I may still find serenity in the act of looking. I feel that if we are bold enough to address the questions head-on, we will be able to move closer to actual life. I do not care whether there is a definitive solution since I think that our goal in life is to confront the questions that arise throughout our lives. We need to look at the philosophical techniques and the principles of intentionality and authenticity that bring existential psychology out of theory and into a practical application of the study of the human mind.

Authenticity, phenomenology, and intentionality are simply the study of phenomena, which is to say, the contents of all things physical and intangible that we experience. To understand the world around us, we must allow all the experiences we have had with our surroundings to speak to us. Interconnectedness between subject and object is intentionality. Existentialism has its roots in subjectivity, so keep that in mind. Phenomenology, on the other hand, is an endeavor to remove oneself from one's own point of view to see things as they truly are. Even if we adhere to the scientific approach, we must still look at the issue from a subjective perspective to understand it. Existentialism accepts this. To understand our existence, existential psychology uses the concept of intentionality.

As we grapple with our deepest issues and the realities of our existence, authenticity may be our greatest difficulty. Existentialists think that we are all living in some degree of denial of our own human potential. If, for example, a person refuses to accept the fact that he or she will die, the person is not completely taking part in the human experience. To avoid confronting our own mortality, we engage specialists to make the dead corpse appear like it is only sleeping. This is obvious in American conventions around death. The most typical way of not living honestly is to live following the norms of society and to follow the crowd. For people, existential psychology is a philosophy that urges them to live their lives following their true selves.

Emotional well-being and human existentialism have always been a concern for existentialists, and spirituality has a significant role to play. It is important to note that a number of influential theologians and philosophers have shaped the history of existential psychology. It is widely accepted that Martin Luther, the reformer, was the first existentialist. Existentialism is often credited to Lutheran minister-turned-philosopher Soren Kierkegaard. Paul Tillich, a Lutheran priest schooled in existential theology and philosophy, is one of our greatest thinkers and theologians. "The Cry for Myth" by Rollo May, a qualified theologian and spiritual director, raises an important topic about the decline in religious spirituality and belief in our society. This is only a small sample of the many ways in which existentialism and religion are intertwined.

It is important to understand how our clients see the infinite because of current existential research in psychology in general and existential psychology. A number of prominent existential psychologists are now conducting research on this subject according to Yalom (1980). For example, researchers are trying to figure out if there are any distinctions in religious and spiritual beliefs and practices among people who profess to be gay or transgender. Another related research topic questions if there are cultural variances in how people perceive God and gender inequalities. In contrast to mainstream psychology, existential psychology must use a more purposeful approach to help clients explore their interactions with a divine higher mind/God. God or gods are not the issue here, but how one perceives and expresses something which is beyond words or one's own understanding. It does not matter whether we identify our spirituality with a religion or a certain belief system.

It has traditionally been left to religion, particularly the Christian church, to discuss this issue. According to McMinn (2011), recent polls showed the number of persons in the United States who identify themselves as members of a church, denomination, or the Christian faith has decreased. Virtue (1998) explained that when Martin Marty prophesied thirty years ago that corporate religion systems and religious affiliation would wane, the Lutheran theologian projected that individuals' spirituality would take over. Individuals, he thought, will draw from a variety of spiritual traditions to build their own distinctive belief system. Experiential psychology is best equipped to help people sort out how their own experiences of the sacred coincide or conflict with their understandings of the Holy. For individuals, finding and owning paradoxes may help them better understand what they want and look for in life.

It might be difficult to talk about the Holy in a non-judgmental way. There are many who believe that investigating an individual's own relationship with God is akin to fostering magical thinking or even dissociation. It is possible that some people may view a psychological or existential psychological approach to spirituality as outside the scope of the discipline. It is true that the loss of myth in our culture has led to the destabilization of our cultural structure. In our daily existence, we all have a built-in need for myth; we must acknowledge something larger than ourselves. We need to experience the "God beyond God" and the sacred as "the foundation of our existence".

According to Yalom (1980), "Being" or "knowing oneself" is what Kierkegaard saw as the first step toward experiencing the divine. To "be" means to exist, to genuinely live, and to show a keen interest in the lives of others. In Kierkegaard's concept of existentialism, he describes the conflict between being and being alive, and the intense interest in another person and the contact with the Holy as existentialist. It is during this chaos that Kierkegaard sees the transcendent, and it is in this messiness that Kierkegaard sees the existentialism. Encouraging people to explore their encounters with

God in a meaningful way will be an important goal for existential psychology, which will benefit the spiritual counseling approach.

Humanistic Psychology (Insights into the Minds of Humans)

Behaviorism and psychoanalysis were the two major schools of thinking until the late 1950s. Some psychologists have been condemned for both their deterministic tendencies and their disregard for human consciousness. Abraham Maslow and Clark Moustakas, among others, embraced the humanistic approach in response. Humanistic psychology is a positive approach that believes that each person's subjective experience is the most essential element in his or her conduct. Principles of humanistic psychology include:

1. Individuals are free to make their own decisions.
2. In order to evolve, people must accept responsibility for their own actions since they have free choice.
3. When it comes to self-actualization, people are naturally drawn to that goal.
4. Human beings are intrinsically good creatures.

As a humanistic psychologist, you do not conduct group research since you treat each patient as a distinct individual with unique experiences.

Transpersonal Psychology (Psychology of the Self)

Humanistic and transpersonal psychology are both based on Abraham Maslow's theory of self-actualization. In contrast to the humanistic approach, transpersonal psychology takes a step further by including the effect of transcendent or spiritual experiences. A greater purpose in life and the attributes of compassion, creativity, wisdom, and unconditional love are looked for by transpersonal psychologists. There are some transpersonal psychologists who regard themselves as facilitators rather than counselors. Their job is to serve as a guide for patients while they search for their own truth. The focus on relationships is another fundamental premise of transpersonal psychology. An individual's mind and how it functions are examined in connection to their interactions with others, including the therapist. Transpersonal philosophy, like the humanistic approach, encourages people to pursue their own personal growth and development.

Spirituality and the Healing Concept

The concept that spirituality can heal has been around for a long time. For thousands of years, people relied on spirituality to treat their ailments. Sickness and health were viewed as the result of the influence of the spirits in early animistic societies. The shaman, a spiritual healer, was the paradigmatic healer in this system. It was customary for shaman practitioners to utilize spiritual therapies to restore the health of members of a tribe who had fallen ill. Today, many cultures still rely on shamans to provide most of their healthcare. A lack of scientific evidence is one of the reasons modern physicians do not give shamans credit. Professor of psychology at the Saybrook Graduate School in San Francisco Dr. Stanley Krippner believes, "They are doing something valuable since they have persisted for millennia."

Echinacea and other herbal remedies are used, but so are rituals and processes that are remarkably like those used in modern psychotherapies. Sophisticated imagery and dream interpretation, together with self-regulation and help from others, are typically used in the healing process of a shaman, according to Krippner. The success rate of shamans can be explained by a variety of factors. Most of us do not think that shamanic rituals truly exorcise bad spirits and illnesses from our bodies. Alternatively, the placebo effect might be to blame. If patients truly feel they will be helped by taking part in a shamanic ceremony, then some of those people will see improvements solely because of their optimistic expectations.

Shamanism, on the other hand, may work for reasons we do not understand, and its healing power still is a mystery. What makes spiritual treatments so successful, whether done by ancient shamans or modern-day therapists, is that they call on our life force: our body's intrinsic urge to survive. Research in body/mind medicine shows that our thoughts, emotions, and behavior may either assist or impede the life force. Spiritual interventions can heal when standard psychotherapy fails because they untie the mental and emotional knots that inhibit the life force from functioning. Religion and spirituality have only lately been studied for their potential to heal. A lot more study is needed to convince insurance companies, therapists, and patients that spiritual growth may have a positive impact on one's mental health.

To put it another way, spirituality is not simply about healing. It is about the astonishment on a child's face, the love we feel for a family member, the freshness of the snow in the forests and fields, and the thrill of soul-stirring music that fills us with peace and happiness. When we perceive the sacred in our lives, we open ourselves to a richer and more meaningful existence. This is what makes our life worth living; these are the moments that fuel our souls.

This book, *Spiritual Integration in Counseling Psychology*, concludes that whether we are aware of it or not, we mix both strategies. It is undeniable that psychology's primary focus has been on alleviating the suffering of the ill and alleviating their mental pain. However, this concentration has meant that the study of happiness and inner peace, as well as pleasant emotions, has been comparatively overlooked until lately. Psychologists may understand how individuals can best improve their lives and strive towards satisfaction and self-development by researching happiness, inner spiritual calm, and pleasant feelings. As a result, we need to incorporate spirituality into our lives, and to integrate the spiritual elements in our psychotherapeutic and mental health programs.

Works Cited

Bailes, F. (2015). *Basic principles of the science of the mind* (2nd ed.) [print]. Devross & Company.

Beattie, M. (1998). *Codependents' guide to the twelve steps* (1st ed.) [print]. Simon and Schuster.

Beck, A. T. (1979). *Cognitive therapy and the emotional disorders* (2nd ed.) [print]. Meridian Publisher.

Benson, H. (2000). *The relaxation response* (1st ed.) [print]. William Morrow Publisher Inc., an imprint of Harpers Collins Publishers.

Burgess, W. (2006). *The bipolar handbook, real life questions with up-to-date answers* (2nd ed.) [print]. Penguin Group.

Burns, D. (1999). *The feeling good handbook* (1st ed.) [print]. Penguin Random House LLC.

Butler-Bowdon, T. (2017). *50 psychology classics, the greatest books distilled* (2nd ed.) [print]. Nicholas Breadley Publishing.

Cohen, L. J. (2016). *The handy psychology answer book* (1st ed.) [print]. Visible Ink Publisher.

Corey, G. (2017). *Theory and practice of counseling and psychotherapy* (1st ed.) [print]. Cengage Learning Publishers.

Gray, P., & Bjorklund, D. F. (2014). *Psychology* (1st ed.) [print]. Worth Publishers.

Hemmings, J. (2018). *How psychology works, applied psychology* (2nd ed.) [print]. Penguin Random House Publishers.

Hoffman, E. (1982). *Develop your psychic skills* (1st ed.) [print]. Schiffer Publishing, Ltd.

Holmes, E. (2005). *Living the science of mind* (2nd ed.) [print]. DeVross and Company Publishers.

Jung, C. G. (2010). *The undiscovered self* (3rd ed.) [print]. Princeton University Press.

Kardek, A. (2004). *Introduction to the spiritist philosophy* (2nd ed.) [print]. Allan Kardec Educational Society Press.

Kelly, E. F., Crabtree, A., & Marshall, P. (2015). *Beyond physicalism, toward reconciliation of science and spirituality* (1st ed.) [print]. Rowman & Littlefield Publishers.

Kluger, J. (2019). *Understanding our own mind / mental health, a new understanding* (1st ed.) [print]. Special Time Magazine Edition, Meredith Publishing Corporation.

Kurtz, E., & Ketcham, K. (2002). *The spirituality of imperfection, storytelling and the search for meaning* (1st ed.) [print]. Bantam Books.

Lipton, B. H. (2016). *The biology of belief, unleashing the power of consciousness, matter and miracles* (1st ed.) [print]. Hay House Inc. Publisher.

Mackenzie, J. (2015). *Psychopath free, recovering from emotionally abusive relationships with narcissists, sociopaths, and other toxic people* (2nd ed.) [print]. Berkley Books.

Masters, P. (2012). *Master's degree curriculum* (2nd ed.) [print]. Burbank Printing.

McMinn, M. R. (2011). *Psychology, theology, and spirituality in christian counseling* (1st ed.) [print]. Tyndale House Publishers Inc.

Miller, W. R. (2013). *Motivational interviewing, helping people change* (3rd ed.) [print]. The Guilford Press.

Morse, M. (2000). *Where God Lives, the science of the paranormal and how our brains are linked to the universe* (1st ed.) [print]. HarperCollins Publishers.

Murphy, J. (2011). *The power of your subconscious mind* (1ˢᵗ ed.) [print]. Penguin Group.

Myers, F. W. (1903). *Human personality and its survival of bodily death* (1ˢᵗ ed.) [print]. Longmans, Green, and Co. Publishers.

Orloff, J. (2000). *Intuitive healing, 5 steps to physical, emotional, and sexual wellness* (2ⁿᵈ ed.) [print]. Random House Inc.

Ponder, C. (1987). *The dynamic laws of prayers* (1ˢᵗ ed.) [Print]. DeVross and Company Publisher.

Solomon, A. (2015). *The noonday demon, an atlas of depression* (1ˢᵗ ed.) [print]. Scribner Publisher.

Virtue, D. (1998). *Divine guidance, how to have a dialogue with God and your guardian angels* (1ˢᵗ ed.) [print]. St. Martin's Griffin Publishers.

Wade, C., Travis, C., & Garry, M. (2014). *Psychology* (3ʳᵈ ed.) [print]. Pearson Publishers.

Yalom, I. D. (1980). *Existential Psychotherapy* (1ˢᵗ ed.) [print]. Basic Books Publishers.

Yalom, I. D. (2002). *The gift of therapy* (2ⁿᵈ ed.) [print]. HarperCollins Publishers.

The Author's Bio

Sam Youssef, Ph.D., PsyThD, M.Sc.

Dr. Sam Youssef is a published author, a researcher, clinician, a doctor of theocentric psychology, and a certified spiritual counselor who is currently a doctoral researcher at Grand Canyon University. His areas of expertise include spiritual counseling psychology, cognitive psychology, metaphysical parapsychology, holistic therapies, medical hypnosis, energy medicine, natural health, and general counseling services to patients who are looking for an integrated approach of psycho-spiritual-somatic treatment programs. He is the author of nine books published in Egypt and the Middle East in the fields of psychology, natural therapies, parapsychology, and philosophy.

He was recognized by the Center of Excellence Academy in England in 2021 with the career achievement award and was also awarded the Outstanding Therapist Award by the same academy in 2020. Dr. Youssef was awarded the Clinician of the Year Award in 2018 by Gentiva Health Care in Indiana, USA. He earned a Doctor of Philosophy degree with emphasis on pastoral counseling psychology from Sedona University in Arizona. He also earned a Doctor of Philosophy degree in parapsychology from the same university, a Master of Science degree with emphasis on neurological rehabilitation from Rosalind Franklin University of Health Sciences/ The Chicago Medical School. Currently, he is pursuing a new Doctor of Philosophy degree in general psychology with emphasis in cognition and instructions from Grand Canyon University.

His long-term professional interests include academic teaching as a professor of general psychology at the university level and continuing his research career. His research goals include studying human behavior and mental thought processes through analyzing the cognitive processes in both the conscious and subconscious mind.

Email: samyoussef21@yahoo.com
Website: http://www.dr
samyoussef.org
http://www.higher
mindcenter.com